COMPUTER

PROGRAMMING FOR KIDS

An Easy Step-By-Step Guide For Beginners

To Learn Programming And Coding Skills

SEAN DAMON

Table of Contents

Introduction 3

Chapter 1: What Is A Programming Language And Popular Programming
Languages 7

Chapter 2: Execution And Statement About A Program 13

Chapter 3: Functions, Input, Output 23

Chapter 4: Web Programming 36

Chapter 5: Object-Oriented Programming 42

Chapter 6: Comparing Deep Learning And Machine Learning 50

Chapter 7: Algorithms In Programming 59

Chapter 8: Working With Inheritance 67

Chapter 9: Syntax 73

Chapter 10: Creating Your First Database 80

Chapter 11: Working With Popular Apps 87

Chapter 12: Exception Handling 96

Chapter 13: Gathering Your Data 102

Conclusion 109

Introduction

Welcome to the world of computer programming for kids, or the act of writing a program to tell your computer what to do. Programs are written using a series of instructions in a particular language, three of which I will be talking about here – Java, SQL, and C++.

Computer programming is not as difficult as it first looks, and it can be a lot of fun, as long as you do it properly. I have prepared a basic "Hello, World!" tutorial for each of the three languages, just to give you an idea of how it all works. Apart from this, I have also enclosed some useful tips for beginners and the common mistakes that newbies tend to make while programming.

Simply, programming environment is a software that will allow you to create, compile, and execute computer programs on the system. It is an interface between the programmer and the computer, which will convert the programs that you will write into the computer's language and ask it to execute the same for you. Therefore, before you pick up any programming language, be sure to enquire about the required programming environment and how the same can be set up on the computer that you intend to use for your programming course.

Digging deeper into the programming environment and its setup, it is made up of three basic elements, namely text editor, compiler, and interpreter. In all probability, you will need all these three components for your course. So, before you go searching for them, let us help you understand what they exactly are and why you will need them.

Text Editor

A text editor is a simple text program that will allow you to create text files in which you will write your code. Depending on the programming language you are working on, the extension of the text file will change, for instance, if you're programming in C language, your text files will have the extension .c.

If you are working on a Windows machine, you can simply search for Notepad in the search bar and use it as a text editor for your programs. You can also explore Notepad++ for some advanced options. It is freely available and you will just need to download and install it on your machine. On the other hand, if you are a Mac user, you can explore text editor options like BBEdit and TextEdit.

Compiler

Now that you have written the program and you are all ready to test if you have written it correctly or not, you have to give it to the computer and see if it understands what you are trying to communicate. However, the computer only understands binary language, and what you have written is far from what it can directly digest. Therefore, this file needs to be converted into a binary format.

If you have made syntactical errors and not followed the rules of the programming language, the compiler will not be able to make this conversion smoothly and will raise an error message for you. Therefore, the compiler is a program that checks if you have followed the syntactical rules of the chosen programming language and converts the text file into its binary form. Moreover, this process of conversion is referred to as compilation.

Most programming languages like C, Java, C++, and Pascal, besides many others, require compilation, and you will need to install their respective compilers before you can execute any programs written using them.

Interpreter

Unlike the programming languages mentioned above, there are some other programming languages like Python and Perl that do not require a compiler. Therefore, instead of a compiler, they need an interpreter, which is also software. The interpreter simply reads the program from the text file and as it parses the file, it converts the contents of the file and executes them. If you are working on any such programming languages, remember to install the corresponding interpreter on your system before starting.

If you haven't worked with a computer before or have little to no experience in installing software on the computer, technical advice from an expert is recommended. However, be sure to do the installation yourself, as it will help you build an acquaintance with the device that you will work with in the near future.

Besides this, if your computer does not support the installation of any of the programming environment elements, you can also make use of the online compilers and interpreters that are available for all the different programming languages nowadays. All you need is a good Internet connection and a web browser to open these online facilities and get started with your programming lessons and practice sessions right away.

1.

What Is a Programming Language and Popular Programming Languages

There are three main categories of computer programming language:

Machine Language

This is the default computer language that is built in primitive instructions represented to the computer in binary code. Thus, if you want to instruct a computer, you must write in binary code. Here is an example of 'hello world' in binary:

01001000 01100101 01101100 01101100 01101111 00100000 01110111 01101111 01110010 01101100 01100100

Assembly Language

Assembly languages are alternatives to machine languages. They use mnemonics to represent machine language instructions. Since computers cannot understand assembly language, we use a program called an assembler to convert assembly language code into machine language code. Compared to machine languages, assembly languages are relatively easier to learn and use, but they are still tedious because they are closer to machine language.

High-Level Programming Languages

The late 1990s ushered in the development of a new generation of computer programming languages called high-level programming languages.

High-level programming languages are English-like computer programming languages that are platform-independent, which means code written in high-level programming language can run on any machine or computer.

Almost every programming language in use in the modern programming world is high-level. These languages use statements to instruct a computer to perform sets of instructions. Here is an example of calculating the sum of two numbers using modern programming languages:

Number1 = 10

Number2 = 100

Sum = Number1 + Number2

Today, we have many high-level programming languages. The list below shows the most popular programming languages, the ones commonly applicable in any field.

- Python

- Java

- C++

- JavaScript

- Ruby

In this guide, we shall be discussing the essentials you need to master to start programming or writing computer code in three programming languages: Java, C++, and Python (version 3).

The next phase starts the discussion by looking at the basic elements, whose understanding of which will allow you to get started on the path to being a proficient programmer.

Programming Basics

Like human languages, high-level programming languages have a set of key elements. Most high-level programming languages have the following core elements:

- Environments

- Keywords

- Data Types

- Variables

- Operators

- Control Flow

- Functions

- Arrays

- Strings

- Inputs/Outputs

Environment Setup

Since computers lack the ability to understand high-level programming languages directly, we use translator or convertor where we write our code and then translate it to machine code. We call this a development environment.

Although it is not a programming element by itself, setting up your development environment is usually the very first step to working with every programming language. It mainly comprises of installing a certain type of software on your computer so that you can create computer code and translate this code into the language your computer can understand.

With most high-level programming languages, the most notable tools necessary to create a conventional programming environment are:

Text Editor

A text editor is a piece of software we use to write computer code in plain text without formatting. Microsoft Windows has Notepad as its default text editor. Source code is the name we use to refer to the Code written and saved by text editor.

Translators

We use translators to convert source code into binary language. The binary code translated then becomes what programmers refer to as 'object code.' Translators can be:

1. **Assemblers:** We use these to convert low-level languages into machine code.

2. **Compilers:** Compilers convert source code to binary code and then execute the binary. If the program runs into an error during the execution process, the compilation stops without creating a binary. The most popular compiled languages are C, C++, Objective-C, Swift, and Pascal.

3. **Interpreters:** Interpreters are similar to compilers but instead of running the entire program, they convert the code line by line. This means that every line of code runs until an error occurs. Once the program returns an error, the interpreter automatically stops and reports the error.

The most popular interpreted languages are Python, Ruby, JavaScript, and Perl.

4. **Hybrid Translators:** Hybrid translators are a combination of compilers and interpreters. They convert the source code into Bytecode. Runtime engines then translate and execute the bytecode. The main example here is Java that uses the Java Virtual Machine (JVM).

NOTE: Set up your programming environment depending on the various instructions given by each of the three programming languages we shall be working with—and each language has different environment setup instructions.

2.

Execution and Statement about a Program

Statement

Statements: What Are They?

Before I begin explaining what a statement is, let me pose you a simple question. When was the last time you had to choose between two things, depending on the elements like what you prefer, what you can afford, what is near, and what isn't? Whenever we make decisions, we take into account quite a few components and elements which will eventually influence our decision accordingly. Similarly, to help us with such issues, we use statements, and that is exactly what we will be looking into.

In the simplest definition, Statements are nothing more than instructions that Program interpreter understands and executes, we have been writing some ourselves when we set values to variables.

Statements, where we assign values to variables, are called assignment statements. However, as long as Program is being discussed, generally, statements refer to 'if' statements.

The 'if' statement is what provides Programs with a situation and allows Program to take appropriate action 'if' a given situation is true, otherwise, it takes another route. Sounds easy and it is actually interesting too. Let us see how we can create our very first 'if' statement.

Here's the situation. A user wishes to sign in using their account. The prompt asks for the passcode only. If the user inputs the right, case-sensitive, passcode, he should be allowed access. If the user enters the wrong password, it should not go through and inform the user that the entered password was incorrect.

To do that, we first need to establish a password. You can either come up with your own pre-defined one or ask the user to create a new passcode and then re-enter it. I leave the choice up to you.

password = input("Create a password: ")

print("Welcome to the portal")

So far, I have only asked the user to enter a password of their choice. If you wish, you can set any string or numbers as a password. Next, I created a little welcome greeting. Now, we shall ask the user to enter their password:

password_check = input("Please enter your password: ")

The only thing worth noting here is that I changed the name of the variable. If you are wondering why, that is because had I used the same variable name; it would have updated the password, instead of comparing it. Since we wish to verify the password, we will need to use a different variable.

Now, the customer has given us two pieces of information. Here, we tell Programming what to do if the password matches.

if password_check == password:

print("Successful! Welcome back!")

There are two things to notice here. Whenever you type in 'if' as your first word, PyCharm will detect that you wish to create an 'if' statement. The color of 'if' will change to denote the same. After 'if,' we need to define our condition. To do that, you may have observed that I used "==" instead of a single equals sign. These signs are called Operators, which we will discuss later. All you need to know here is this:

'=' is used to assign a value

'==' is used to either equate two variables or compare to see if the two are exactly the same.

In the above instance, we will use this comparison operator. Here is the most interesting bit; unlike all the codes we wrote so far, this line ends with a colon ':'.

Every conditional statement, such as the 'if' statement, ends with a colon in Program to create a block of code that will execute under that colon.

The next line will begin with an indentation. Do not remove that indent as that would cause confusion since I had already set the condition, which quite literally reads as "If password_check is exactly the same as password" and now I added the command that it needs to carry out if the condition is met. When you execute this program, you will begin with the prompt asking you to choose a password. That would be stored as a variable named password. Next, the prompt will ask us to type in the password once again for verification or for login purposes. Whatever we type here will be stored in a variable called password_check. Now, Programs will compare the two values and see if the two are exactly alike. If so, it will print out a success message.

I am quite sure that you have just tried to enter the wrong password deliberately. It ended the program altogether without any warning, right? There is a reason for that. We have only defined the 'if' condition. We never got to the part to define the 'else' condition.

The 'else' condition is the final condition, and it usually comes into play when the 'if' condition or others are not true and are not fulfilled. To do that, we will add two lines of code beneath the first one. Now, the entire program should look like this:

password = input("Create a password: ")

print("Welcome to the portal")

password_check = input("Please enter your password: ")

```
if password_check == password:
```

```
print("Successful! Welcome back!")
```

```
else:
```

```
print("Sorry buddy! That's a Nay!")
```

Notice how 'else' statement needs no indentation here, and it does not require you to provide additional conditions either.

Now, I will run the code twice. Once correct and the other incorrect, let us see how it works:

Correct password

Create a password: 123

Welcome to the portal

Please enter your password: 123

Successful! Welcome back!

Incorrect password

Create a password: 123

Welcome to the portal

Please enter your password: 122

Sorry buddy! That's a Nay!

Here's a question, what if there is more than one condition to a statement? Suppose you are to choose a number between one to three and then give an appropriate message, depending on the number the user chooses, how would we do that?

```
print("Welcome to my little game")

number = int(input("Choose a number between 1-3: "))

if number == 1:

print("You love to consider yourself a leader, don't you?")

elif number == 2:

print("You hate being alone, right?")

elif number == 3:

print("The more, the merrier, is it?")

else:

print("Really? You can't follow simple instructions, can you?")
```

Quite a familiar way to put things, but the only thing to note here is the 'elif' statement. The 'elif' sits right between 'if' and 'else' where 'if' is the first condition, and 'else' is when no conditions are met.

Yes, I know! It should've been named as 'ifel,' but then again, it is what it is!

Try it out yourself, check each of these with various numbers as your picks. For a little fun, use any number greater than three and see what happens.

This is how Programs handles conditional statements. If you are a bit of a gamer, you may have seen various games where decisions can influence the outcome of the game itself. Now you know the culprit!

There is no limit to the number of 'elif' statements. You can create as many as you like. With that said, let's make this a little more interesting.

Nested Conditional ('if') statements

Let us assume that we use the same numbers as above, but this time, we wish to add an 'if' statement within an 'if' statement. Let's imagine that we want out user to select another numeric value, this time in decimal numbers, only if the user decides to choose the first value as the number.

Have a look at the code below and try to find out how the code will be executed.

```
print("Welcome to my little game")

number = int(input("Choose a number between 1-3: "))

if number == 1:
```

print("You love to consider yourself a leader, don't you?")

number2 = float(input("Enter a number with a decimal figure between 1 and 2: "))

if number2 == 2.00:

print("Okay! I meant a little lesser than that!")

elif number < 1.50:

print("Oh, come on! You can go higher!")

else:

print("You know what, forget it!")

 elif number == 2:

print("You hate being alone, right?")

elif number == 3:

print("The more, the merrier, is it?")

else:

print("Really? You can't follow simple instructions, can you?")

We created another variable within the first condition. If the user decides to settle for one, the prompt will ask the user to enter another number. We used the conversion here to convert the incoming number to afloat, as it will have a decimal figure.

We then created another condition which defines the upper limit and the lower limit. To add a little fun to it, there is no correct number to choose from here. Regardless of what the user may choose, they will either receive a message to state that they went a little too high, or one that will encourage them to go higher. The rest will always leave the user in a bit of a puzzled state.

This kind of conditional statement within a conditional statement is called a Nested Statement. This entire block of code can be avoided if the user decides to go for any other number than the triggering point.

Execution

When it comes to programming, iteration means the repetition of lines of code. It's an essential property in computer programming that helps find solutions to problems. Iteration and conditional execution are the main stems of algorithm development.

Let us start with the:

While Statement

Say you want to write a program that can count to 10,000, how will you approach this problem? Will you sit down and write 10,000 printing statements? Although you can, that is going to consume a lot of your time. However, counting is frequent in computers, in fact, computers can count extraordinary values. So, there must be a way out. What you need to do is to print the value of a variable, and repeat the process until you reach 10,000. The method of executing the same code repeatedly is known as looping. Program language has two special statements, while and for, that handle iteration.

3.

Functions, Input, Output

Functions

In this phase, you will know how to write functions easily in a program. Functions are a line of codes, which are designed to perform a particular job. When you want to write a program that will perform a specific task, then you have to define the function and call the function. Furthermore, I will teach you how to pass information to functions and display them on the screen.

At times, the best way to explain a thing is to provide an example. The program below is a welcome program that prints a message.

```
def welcome_user():

" " " Transmit a Welcome Message."""

Print ("Welcome to Learning  Programming.")

welcome_user()
```

In this example, it shows the simplest structure of how a function works. The first line uses the keyword "def" to tell the interpreter that you want to define a function. Therefore, whenever you see the word "def" and the word following it, it signifies a function definition. The parenthesis does the job of holding the information you need. Then after the parentheses, the function definition ends with a colon.

Whenever you see an indented line after defining a function, which is the body of the function. The second line is known as a docstring, although it is a comment and describes the purpose of the function. Docstring is usually enclosed with three quotes. Furthermore, the third line prints the statement "Welcome to Learning Programming." This line contains the main message of the function. This means the welcome user has the primary job of printing "Welcome to Learning Programming."

If you want to call a function, you have to write the function name before following it with parentheses and a colon. Our program output will be as follow:

```
Welcome to Learning Programming.
```

How to Pass Information to a Function

We will modify our example to explain how you can pass information to a function. We can do it in such a way that the program will not only say "Welcome to Learning Programming" but also include the user name. To do that, we have to request a user to enter their name.

```
def welcome user(name):

"""Transmit a Welcome Message."""

Print ("Welcome to Learning Programming, {name.title()}!")

welcome user("Thomas")
```

When we enter welcome user ("Thomas"), it calls the function welcome user() and passes the name "Thomas" to the function to execute the print command. With this, our output will be:

```
Welcome to Learning Programming, Thomas!
```

Arguments and Parameters

We defined a function, which requires the user to input a value for the variable username. Immediately, you call the function and assign a value to it; it prints the message in the print() function. Our function has a variable inside it. The variable is an example of what a parameter is in Program, whereas Thomas is the argument. Arguments are values that contained information and pass from a function call to the function. For instance, when we call the function, we placed a value inside the function. In this scenario, our argument is "Thomas," and we passed the information to the function.

Note: people interchangeably use both terms. Therefore, when you see a definition of a function referred to as an argument or vice-versa.

How to Pass an Argument in Program

Since a function definition can have several parameters, a function call may also require several arguments. It means you can pass your argument to a function in multiple ways. You can use either keyword argument or positional arguments. In the latter, the argument must be of the same order as your parameter, whereas, in the former, each argument comprises a variable name and its equivalent value.

Positional Arguments

This argument is the simplest way of passing an argument in Program because each argument in the function must match with a parameter in the function declaring section. To see how this works, let us write a program that shows information about animals. The function in this situation tells us the particular type of animal and the name of the pet.

```
def animal_list(animal_kind, pet_name):
```

```
""""" Display Details About Animal."""""

print(f "\nThis is a {animal_kind}.")

print (f "My {animal_kind}'s name is {pet_name.title()}.")

animal_list ("Cat," "Lucy")
```

The first block of line defines a function. It indicates that the function requires a particular animal's type and its pet name. After defining the function, we provided the animal kind and pet name. For instance, in the function call (animal_list), we assign Cat as animal kind while Lucy is the pet's name. Our output will display the detail about the animal Cat with the pet name Lucy.

```
This is a Cat.

My Cat's name is Lucy.
```

Calling Multiple Functions

We can call the function as many times as we want. All we need is to add another parameter to our function. Check the code below:

```
def animal_list(animal_kind, pet_name):

""""" Display Details About Animal."""""

print(f "\nThis is a {animal_kind}.")

print (f "My {animal_kind}'s name is {pet_name.title()}.")

animal_list ("Cat", "Lucy")

animal_list ("Dog," "Bruce")

animal_list ("Rat," "Chase")
```

The program follows the same sequence and performs the output. However, in this situation, we added two more parameters to the list. Therefore, our output will look like this:

```
This is a Cat.

My Cat's name is Lucy.

This is a Dog.

My Dog's name is Bruce.
```

This is a Rat.

My Rat's name is Chase.

Calling a function several times is an efficient way when you have several parameters. The code about the details of the animal is written once inside the function. However, whenever you want to describe a new animal, all you need is to call the function by providing information about the animal.

Keyword Arguments

This is a name/value pair, which you pass to a function. You have to directly link the value and the variable name inside the argument. With this, there won't be any confusion when you pass the argument to the function. Let's rewrite our previous code using the keyword arguments to call our animal_list()

```python
def animal_list(animal_kind, pet_name):

""""" Display Details About Animal."""""

print(f "\nThis is a {animal_kind}.")

print (f "My {animal_kind}'s name is {pet_name.title()}.")
```

```
animal_list (animal_kind ="Cat", pet_name= "Lucy")

animal_list (pet_name= "Chase", animal_kind ="Rat")
```

Our first four lines haven't changed. However, there is a difference between the last two lines. When the interpreter reads the fourth line, it calls the function and assigns the parameter Cat to animal_kind and Lucy to pet_name, respectively. For the next line, it will perform the same operation because the order doesn't matter when dealing with keyword arguments. Therefore, the last two lines of codes are equivalent and produce the same output. Our program above will display:

```
This is a Cat.

My Cat's name is Lucy.

This is a Rat.

My Rat's name is Chase.
```

When using keyword arguments, ensure that the right parameter names are used in the function definition to avoid any error.

Default Value

Besides using the keyword parameter and position argument, each parameter can have a default value in a function. If you provide a parameter that is providing in the function, Program uses the value. However, if there is no parameter value, then Program uses a default value for the parameter.

```
def animal_list(pet_name, animal_kind = "Cat"):

""""" Display Details About Animal.""""

print(f "\nThis is a {animal_kind}.")

print (f "My {animal_kind}'s name is {pet_name.title()}.")

animal_list (pet_name= "Lucy")
```

Compare this program with the previous code. Did you notice anything from the first and last line? Well, animal_list function is used to describe a particular animal kind where we set the default value as Cat.

```
I have a Cat.

My name is Lucy.
```

Observe that the parameter order inside the function definition must be changed since the default value makes it pointless to stipulate the particular animal kind as an argument. Therefore, the only argument available in the function is the name of the pet.

Basic Functions for Interactivity

In this phase, we will name the two most important functions for interactivity in Program, which are print(), standard output, on the other hand, the standard input is input(), which we will explain below.

Standard Output

The print() function is used to display information by the standard output that normally corresponds to the computer screen.

In Program2, print is a reserved word, while in Program3, print() is a function, so the content will be expressed as a parameter within a function, or, said in another way, must be in parentheses.

```
interactivity.py ✕

1    print("Output")
2    print("The end")
3
```

As we can see in this simple example, we make use of print and should appear in console two strings, both "Output" and "The end".

It is important to note that there are many occasions in which you have two variables that are strings, and sometimes, it is necessary to use both in the same print; therefore, we proceed to concatenate and print the two strings of characters together.

Standard Input

For Program3, the default function is input(), which is responsible for obtaining some input value entered by the user, it will have to be assigned to a variable, so you get a string. An important feature of this function is that you can also show a message on the screen, thus achieving to show users what they have to enter and that the programmer can write a message so that it tells what type of data has to be entered, for example, to tell the user that needs to enter a natural number for the calculation of the area of a rectangle, but to understand a little better this, it is important to look at the following example:

```
interactivity.py ×

1    var1=input("Put a number:")
2
```

In this example, we see that the variable that was initialized, var1, is equal to the entry that the user enters, it should be a number, since the function specifies the user to enter a number, the same entry is going to become a string, because the function input(), always return a string, and from there, you can make the calculations.

Escape characters: These are some types of character combinations, which behave differently within the strings, as they allow us to do things we cannot do easily, such as a line break.

\\	\
\'	'
\"	"
\a	Sound
\b	ASCII regression
\f	Page advance
\n	Line break
\r	Carry Return
\t	Horizontal Tabulation
\v	Vertical Tabulation
\ooo	Octal value character
\xhh	Hexadecimal value character

Triple Quotes: They are used to place multiline character strings, this can be done with single triple quotes "'text'", or triple double quotes """text""" an example of its use is as follows:

```
interactivity.py ×

1    string='''Hi
2    how are
3    you
4    '''
5    string2= """This
6    is
7    a
8    example"""
9    print(string+string2)
10
```

In this example, we created the two variables, string and string2, we used both the triple single quotes and the triple-double quotes, in which we placed several line breaks, without the need to make escape characters, in this case without the \n. Finally, we will print on the screen the concatenation of the variable string and string2.

4.

Web Programming

This phase briefly explains web programming. The Internet is a basic entity for cores of people now. Explanation of web modularity with Program can help you to learn the subject better.

HTTP Communication Protocol

Communication is a wonderful thing. It allows information to be passed between individuals. The animals send out the chemical element and mating messages. People say sweet things to express their love to their lovers. The hunters whistled and quietly rounded up their prey. The waiter barked to the kitchen for two sets of fried chicken and beer. Traffic lights direct traffic, television commercials broadcast, and the Pharaoh's pyramids bear the curse of forbidden entry. With communication, everyone is connected to the world around them. In the mysterious process of communication, the individuals involved always abide by a specific protocol. In our daily conversation, we use a set grammar. If two people use different grammars, then they communicate with different protocols, and eventually, they don't know what they're talking about.

Communication between computers is the transfer of information between different computers. Therefore, computer communication should also follow the Communication Protocol Conference. In order to achieve multi-level global Internet communication, computer communication also has a multi-level protocol system. HTTP Protocol is the most common type of network protocol. Its full name is the Hypertext Transfer Protocol.

The HTTP protocol enables the transfer of files, especially hypertext. In the Internet age, it is the most widely used Internet Protocol. In fact, when we visit a Web site, we usually type an HTTP URL into the browser, such as http://www.google.com, for example, it says that you need to use the HTTP protocol to access your site.

HTTP works as a fast-food order:

1. **Request:** A customer makes a request to the waiter for a chicken burger.
2. **Response:** The server responds to the request of the customer according to the situation.

Depending on the situation, the waiter may respond in a number of ways, such as:

- The waiter prepares the Drumstick Burger and hands it to the customer. (Everything is OK)

- The waitress found herself working at the dessert stand. He sent his customers to the official counter to take orders. (Redirects)

- The waiter told the customer that the Drumstick hamburger was out. (Cannot be found)

When the transaction is over, the waiter puts the transaction behind him and prepares to serve the next customer.

GET /start.html HTTP/3.0

Host: www.mywebsite.com

In the starting line, there are three messages:

- Get method. Describes the operation that you want the server to perform.

- / start. The path to the html resource. These points to the index on the server. HTML file.

- HTTP 3.0. The first widely used version of HTTP was 3.0, and the current version is 3.3.

The early HTTP protocol had only the GET method. Following the HTTP protocol, the server receives the GET request and passes the specific resource to the client. This is similar to the process of ordering and getting a Burger from a customer. In addition to the GET method, the most common method is the POST method. It is used to submit data from the client to the server, with the data to be submitted appended to the request. The server does some processing of the data submitted by the POST method. The sample request has a header message. The type of header information is Host, which indicates the address of the server you want to access.

After receiving the request, the server will generate a response to the request, such as:

HTTP/3.0 200 OK

Content-type: text/plain

Content-length: 10

Jesus Christ

The first line of the reply contains three messages:

- HTTP 3.0: Protocol version

- 200: Status Code

- Ok: Status Description

OK is a textual description of the status code 200, which is just for human readability. The computer only cares about three-digit status codes. Status Code, which is 200 here. 200 means everything is OK, and the resource returns normally. The status code represents the class that the server responded to.

There are many other common status codes, such as:

- 302, Redirect: I don't have the resources you're looking for here, but I know another place where xxx does. You can find it there.

- 404, Not Found: I can't find the resources you're looking for.

The next line, Content-type, indicates the type of resource that the body contains. Depending on the type, the client can start different handlers (such as displaying image files, playing sound files, and so on). Content-length indicates the length of the body part, in bytes. The rest is the body of the reply, which contains the main text data.

Through an HTTP transaction, the client gets the requested resource from the server, which is the text here. The above is a brief overview of how the HTTP protocol works, omitting many details. From there, we can see how Program communicates with HTTP.

http.client Package

The client package can be used to make HTTP requests. As we saw, some of the most important information for HTTP requests are the host address, request method, and resource path. Just clarify this information, plus HTTP. With the help of the client package, you can make an HTTP request.

Here is the code below in Python:

```python
import http.client

connection = http.client.HTTPConnection("www.facebook.com") #hostaddress conn.request("POST", "/") # requestmethod and resource path

response = connection.getresponse() # Gets a response

print(response.status, response.reason)# Replies with status code and description

content = response.read()
```

5.

Object-Oriented Programming

W̲e are now going to look at the four concepts of object-oriented programming and how they apply to Python.

Inheritance

The first major concept is called "inheritance." This refers to things being able to derive from another. Let's take sports cars, for instance. All sports cars are vehicles, but not all vehicles are sports cars. Moreover, all sedans are vehicles, but all vehicles are not sedans, and sedans are certainly not sports cars, even though they're both vehicles.

So basically, this concept of Object-Oriented programming says that things can and should be chopped up into as small and fine of precise concepts as possible.

In Python, this is done by deriving classes.

Let's say we had another class called SportsCar.

```
class Vehicle(object):

    def__init__(self, makeAndModel, prodYear, airConditioning):
```

```
        self.makeAndModel = makeAndModel

        self.prodYear = prodYear

        self.airConditioning = airConditioning

        self.doors = 4

    def honk(self):

        print "%s says: Honk! Honk!" % self.makeAndModel
```

Now, below that, create a new class called SportsCar, but instead of deriving object, we're going to derive from Vehicle.

```
class SportsCar(Vehicle)

    def__init__(self, makeAndModel, prodYear, airConditioning):

        self.makeAndModel = makeAndModel

        self.prodYear = prodYear

        self.airConditioning = airConditioning

        self.doors = 4
```

Leave out the honk function, we only need the constructor function here. Now declare a sports car. I'm just going to go with the Ferrari.

```
ferrari = SportsCar("Ferrari Laferrari", 2016, True)
```

Now test this by calling

ferrari.honk()

and then saving and running. It should go off without a hitch.

Why is this? This is because the notion of inheritance says that a child class derives functions and class variables from a parent class. Easy enough concept to grasp. The next one is a little tougher.

Polymorphism

The idea of polymorphism is that the same process can be performed in different ways depending upon the needs of the situation. This can be done in two different ways in Python: method overloading and method overriding.

Method overloading is defining the same function twice with different arguments. For example, we could give two different initializer functions to our Vehicle class. Right now, it just assumes a vehicle has 4 doors. If we wanted to specifically say how many doors a car had, we could make a new initializer function below our current one with an added doors argument, like so (the newer one is on the bottom):

```python
def __init__(self, makeAndModel, prodYear, airConditioning):

    self.makeAndModel = makeAndModel

    self.prodYear = prodYear
```

```
        self.airConditioning = airConditioning

        self.doors = 4

def __init__(self, makeAndModel, prodYear, airConditioning, doors):

self.makeAndModel = makeAndModel

self.prodYear = prodYear

self.airConditioning = airConditioning

self.doors = doors
```

Somebody now, when creating an instance of the Vehicle class, can choose whether they define the number of doors or not. If they don't, the number of doors is assumed to be 4.

Method overriding is when a child class overrides a parent class's function with its code.

To illustrate, create another class which extends Vehicle called Moped. Set the doors to 0, because that's absurd, and set air conditioning to false. The only relevant arguments are make/model and production year. It should look like this:

```
class Moped(Vehicle):

    def __init__(self, makeAndModel, prodYear):
```

self.makeAndModel = makeAndModel

self.prodYear = prodYear

self.airConditioning = False

self.doors = 0

Now, if we made an instance of the Moped class and called the honk() method, it would honk. But it is common knowledge that mopeds don't honk, they beep. So let's override the parent class's honk method with our own. This is super simple. We just redefine the function in the child class:

def honk(self):

print "%s says: Beep! Beep!" % self.makeAndModel

I'm part of the 299,000,000 Americans who couldn't name a make and model of Moped if their life depended on it, but you can test out if this works for yourself but declaring an instance of the Moped class and trying it out.

Abstraction

The next major concept in object-oriented programming is abstraction. This is the notion that the programmer and user should be far from the inner workings of the computer. This has two benefits.

The first is that it decreases the inherent security risks and the possibility for catastrophic system errors, by either human or otherwise. By abstracting the programmer from the inner workings of the computer like memory and the CPU and often even the operating system, there's a low chance of any sort of mishap causing irreversible damage.

The second is that the abstraction innately makes the language easier to understand, read, and learn. Though it makes the language a tad bit less powerful by taking away some of the power that the user has over the entire computer architecture, this is traded instead for the ability to program quickly and efficiently in the language, not wasting time dealing with trivialities like memory addresses or things of the like.

These apply in Python because, well, it's incredibly simple. You can't get down into the nitty-gritty of the computer, or do much with memory allocation or even specifically allocate an array size too easily, but this is a tradeoff for amazing readability, a highly secure language in a highly secure environment, and ease of use with programming. Compare the following snippet of code from C:

```
#include <stdio.h>

int main(void) {

printf("hello world");

return 0;
```

}

to the Python code for doing the same:

print "hello world"

That's it. That's all there is to it.

Abstraction is generally a net positive for a large number of applications that are being written today, and there's a reason Python and other object-oriented programming languages are incredibly popular.

Encapsulation

The last major concept in object-oriented programming is that of encapsulation. This one's the easiest to explain. This is the notion that common data should be put together, and that code should be modular. I'm not going to spend long explaining this because it's a super simple concept. The entire notion of classes is as concise of an example as you can get for encapsulation: common traits and methods are bonded together under one cohesive structure, making it super easy to create things of the sort without having to create a ton of super-specific variables for every instance.

Well, there we go. We finally made it to the end of our little Python adventure. First, I'd like to say thank you for making it through to the end of Python for Beginners: The Ultimate Guide to Python Programming. Let's hope it was informative and able to provide you with all of the tools you need to achieve your goals, whatever they may be.

The next procedure is to use this knowledge. Whether as a hobby or a career move, by learning the basics of Python, you just made one of the best decisions of your life, and your goal now should be finding ways to use it in your day-to-day life to make life easier or to accomplish things you've wanted to accomplish for a long while.

6.

Comparing Deep Learning and Machine Learning

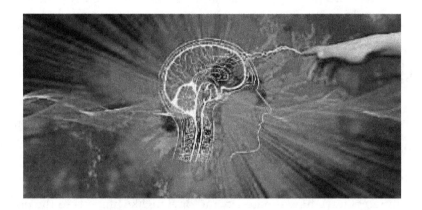

A rtificial intelligence is a field of study that has come up in many conversations for years. A few years ago, this was a futuristic concept that was propagated in movies and comic books. Through years of development and research, we are currently experiencing the best of artificial intelligence. In fact, it is widely expected that AI will help us usher in the new frontier in computing.

Artificial intelligence might share some similarities with Machine Learning and Deep Learning, but they are not the same thing. Many people use these terms interchangeably without considering the ramifications of their assumptions. Deep Learning and Machine Learning are knowledge branches of artificial intelligence. While there are different definitions that have been used in the past to explain artificial intelligence, the basic convention is that this is a process where computer programs are built with the capacity to operate and function like a normal human brain would.

The concept of AI is to train a computer to think the same way a human brain thinks and functions. In as far as the human brain is concerned, we are yet to fully grasp the real potential of our brains. Experts believe that even the most brilliant individuals in the world are unable to fully exhaust their brain capacity.

This, therefore, creates a conundrum, because if we are yet to fully understand and test the limits of our brains, how can we then build computing systems that can replicate the human brain? What happens if computers learn how to interact and operate like humans to the point where they can fully use their brainpower before we learn how to use ours?

Ideally, the power behind AI or the limits of its thinking capacity is yet to be established. However, researchers and other experts in the field have made great strides over the years. One of the closest examples of AI that espouses these values is Sophia. Sophia is probably the most advanced AI model in the world right now. Perhaps given our inability to fully push the limits of our brains, we might never fully manage to push the limits of AI to a point where they can completely replace humans.

Machine Learning and Deep Learning are two branches of artificial intelligence that have enjoyed significant research and growth over the years. The attention towards these frameworks especially comes from the fact that many of the leading tech companies in the world have seamlessly implemented them in their products, and integrated them into human existence. You interact with these models all the time on a daily basis.

Machine Learning and Deep Learning do share a number of features, but they are not the same. Just as is the case with comparing these two with artificial intelligence. In your capacity as a beginner, it is important to learn the difference between these studies, so that you can seek and find amazing opportunities that you can exploit and use to further your skills in the industry. In a world that is continually spiraling towards increased machine dependency, there are many job openings in Machine Learning and Deep Learning at the moment. There will be so much more in the near future too, as people rush to adapt and integrate these systems into their daily operations and lives.

Deep Learning vs. Machine Learning

Before we begin, it is important that you remind yourself of the basic definitions or explanations of these two subjects. Machine Learning is a branch of artificial intelligence that uses algorithms to teach machines how to learn. Further from the algorithms, the Machine Learning models need input and output data from which they can learn through interaction with different users.

When building such models, it is always advisable to ensure that you build a scalable project that can take new data when applicable and use it to keep training the model and boost its efficiency. An efficient Machine Learning model should be able to self-modify without necessarily requiring your input, and still provide the correct output. It learns from structured data available and keeps updating itself.

Deep Learning is a class of Machine Learning that uses the same algorithms and functions used in Machine Learning. However, Deep Learning introduces layered computing beyond the power of algorithms. Algorithms in Deep Learning are used in layers, with each layer interpreting data in a different way. The algorithm network used in Deep Learning is referred to as Artificial Neural Networks.

The Name Artificial Neural Networks gives us the closest iteration of what happens in Deep Learning frameworks. The goal here is to try and mimic the way the human brain functions, by focusing on the neural networks. Experts in Deep Learning Sciences have studied and referenced different studies on the human brain over the years, which has helped spearhead research into this field.

Problem Solving Approaches

Let's consider an example to explain the difference between Deep Learning and Machine Learning.

Say you have a database that contains photos of trucks and bicycles. How can you use Machine Learning and Deep Learning to make sense of this data? At first glance, what you will see is a group of trucks and bicycles. What if you need to identify photos of bicycles separately from trucks using these two frameworks?

To help your Machine Learning algorithm identify the photos of trucks and bicycles based on the categories requested, you must first teach it what these photos are about. How does the Machine Learning algorithm figure out the difference? After all, they almost look alike.

The solution is in a structured data approach. First, you will label the photos of bicycles and trucks in a manner that defines different features that are unique to either of these items. This is sufficient data for your Machine Learning algorithm to learn from. Based on the input labels, it will keep learning and refine its understanding of the difference between trucks and bicycles as it encounters more data. From this simple illustration, it will keep searching through millions of other data it can access to tell the difference between trucks and bicycles.

How Do We Solve This Problem in Deep Learning?

The approach in Deep Learning is different from what we have done in Machine Learning. The benefit here is that in Deep Learning, you do not need any labelled or structured data to help the model identify trucks from bicycles.

The artificial neural networks will identify the image data through the different algorithm layers in the network. Each of the layers will identify and define a specific feature in the photos. This is the same method that our brains use when we try to solve some problems.

Generally, the brain considers a lot of possibilities, ruling out all the wrong ones before settling on the correct one. Deep Learning Models will pass queries through several hierarchical processes to find the solution. At each identification level, the deep neural networks recognize some identifiers that help in distinguishing bicycles from trucks.

This is the simplest way to understand how these two systems work. Both Deep Learning and Machine Learning, however, might not necessarily be applicable methods to tell these photos apart. As you learn about the differences between these two fields, you must remember that you have to define the problem correctly, before you can choose the best approach to implement in solving it. You will learn how to choose the right approach at a later stage in your journey into Machine Learning, which has been covered in the advanced books in this series.

From the example illustrated above, we can see that Machine Learning Algorithms need structured data to help them tell the difference between trucks and bicycles. From this information, they can then produce the correct output after identifying the classifiers.

In Deep Learning, however, your model can identify images of the trucks and bicycles by passing information through several data processing layers in its framework. There is no need for structured data.

To make the correct prediction, Deep Learning Frameworks depend on the output provided at every data processing layer. This information then builds up and presents the final outcome. In this case, it rules out all possibilities to remain with the only credible solution.

From our illustrations above, we have learned some important facts that will help you distinguish Deep Learning from Machine Learning as you learn over the years. We can summarize this in the following points:

Data Presentation

The primary difference between Machine Learning and Deep Learning is evident in the way we introduce data into the respective models. With Machine Learning Models, you will almost always need to use structured data. However, in Deep Learning, the networks depend on artificial neural network layers to identify unique features that help to identify the data.

Algorithms and Human Intervention

The emphasis of Machine Learning is to learn from interacting with different inputs and use patterns. From such interaction, Machine Learning Models can produce better output the longer it learns, and the more interaction it receives. To aid this cause, you must also try to provide as many new data as possible.

When you realize that the output presented is not what you needed, you must retrain the Machine Learning Model to deliver a better output.

Therefore, for a system that should work without human intervention, you will still have to be present from time to time.

In Deep Learning, your presence is not needed. All the nested layers within the neural networks process data at different levels. In the process, however, the model might encounter errors and learn from them.

This is the same way that the human brain works. As you grow up, you learn a lot of important life skills through trial and error. By making mistakes, your brain learns the difference between positive and negative feedback, and you strive to achieve positive results whenever you can.

To be fair, even in Deep Learning, your input will still be required. You cannot confidently assume that the output will always be perfect. This particularly applies when your input data is insufficient for the kind of output you demand from the model.

The underlying factor here is that both Machine Learning and Deep Learning must all use data. The quality of data you have will make a lasting impact on the results you get from these models. Speaking of data, you cannot just use any data you come across. To use either of these models effectively, you must learn how to inspect data and make sure you are using the correct format for the model you prefer.

Machine Learning Algorithms will often need labelled, structured data. For this reason, they are not the best option if you need to find solutions to sophisticated problems that need massive chunks of data.

In the example we used to identify trucks from bicycles, we tried to solve a very simple issue in a theoretical concept. In the real world, however, Deep Learning models are applied in more complex models. If you think about the processes involved, from the concepts to hierarchical data handling and the different number of layers that data must pass through, using Deep Learning models to solve simple problems would be a waste of resources.

While all these classes of AI need data to help in conducting the intelligence we require, Deep Learning models need significantly wider access to data than Machine Learning Algorithms. This is important because Deep Learning Algorithms must prove beyond a reasonable doubt that the output is perfect before it is passed.

7.

Algorithms in Programming

While variables are the data stores in programming, algorithms are the building blocks. It is through algorithms that the software you use can fetch the data you need. Algorithms are the bridge between normal language and computer language. Your challenges are translated into the unique language running your software, before it is translated back to a language you can understand and interpret.

The easiest way to conceptualize an algorithm is a cooking recipe. Recipes outline every procedure of the way from food preparation to the point the meal is ready to serve. This is what algorithms do. They outline the necessary procedures your computer must follow to achieve your intended goals.

While still on the recipe example, in programming, we would refer to recipes as procedures, ingredients as inputs, and the final outcome of your recipe as an output. Algorithms describe how to perform a task, and each time that algorithm is executed, your computer will perform it in the same manner.

To prevent confusion, we must mention that algorithms are not computer code. Algorithms are written in plain language that you understand. It could be English, Korean, Chinese, you name it. Algorithms are precise and have three sections: the start, the middle, and the end. When writing an algorithm, you will actually indicate start for the first procedure, and end for the last procedure.

Algorithms must only include the necessary information to complete a task. They must be precise so that they lead you to an efficient solution. When writing algorithms, it is wise to number your procedures, though it is not mandatory. Some programmers use pseudo-code, a semi-programming language that explains the procedures followed in an algorithm.

Here is an example of an algorithm that requests user email addresses:

- **Procedure 1:** Start
- **Procedure 2:** Create variable to receive user email address
- **Procedure 3:** Clear variable if not empty
- **Procedure 4:** Request user email address
- **Procedure 5:** Store response in variable
- **Procedure 6:** Verify if email address is valid
- **Procedure 7:** Invalid address? Back to Procedure 3
- **Procedure 8:** End

Here is an example of an algorithm that adds two numbers:

Procedure 1: Start

Procedure 2: Declare variables num3, num4 also sum.

Procedure 3: Read variables num3 and num4.

Procedure 4: Add num3 to num4 and assign result to sum.

sum←num3+num4

Procedure 5: Display sum

Procedure 6: End

Here is an algorithm that determines the largest of three values:

Procedure 1: Start

Procedure 2: Declare the variables x, y and z.

Procedure 3: Read variables x, y and z.

Procedure 4: If x>y

If x>z

Display x is largest number.

Else

Display z is largest number.

Else

If y>z

Display y is the largest number.

Else

Display z is largest number.

Procedure 5: End

This is how simple algorithms are. They state what you need in the procedure. A good algorithm must have the following features:

- Clear and precise definition of the input and output.

- All Procedures must be simple and clear.

- The chosen algorithm should be the most effective way to arrive at a solution.

- There should be no computer code in an algorithm.

There are several classes of algorithms and data structures that you need to learn about in programming. You will use them almost everywhere in developmental and competitive programming. Here are the main algorithms:

Sort Algorithms

This is one of the largest categories of algorithms that you will learn in programming. These algorithms allow you to arrange a list in the desired order. Each programming language today comes with its own sorting library. However, it is still important to learn about these:

- Merge sort

- Counting sort

- Heap sort

- Bucket sort

- Quick sort

The knowledge of these algorithms is not enough. What is more important is knowing how, where, and when they are necessary.

Search Algorithms

There are two popular types of search algorithms: breadth-first search as used in group data structures and binary search used in linear data structures. Binary searches are recommended when you need an efficient search on a dataset that is sorted. The concept here is to continually halve the dataset until you narrow your options down to a solitary item. A common use of this algorithm is when you search for the name of a film in an assorted list of movies. The algorithm conducts a binary search by string matching to deliver the right result.

The search algorithm comes in handy in your map when you need to find the shortest possible route from one point to the other, especially if you have many options. It is also used to create intelligent bots in AI. Search engines are some of the biggest users of search algorithms, by trawling the internet for appropriate results before they are displayed.

String Matching and Parsing

One of the biggest problems you will solve in your life as a software programmer is pattern searching and matching. To do this, you need proper knowledge of the following:

- **String matching (KMP algorithm)**

The Knuth-Morris-Pratt (KMP) algorithm is applicable in instances where you need to match short patterns in long strings. One common example is executing a Ctrl+F command for a keyword. Basically, what you are doing is pattern matching the keyword pattern all through the document.

- **String parsing (Regular expression)**

You will also learn to parse over predefined restrictions to validate strings in development, especially for parsing and matching URLs in web development.

Hashing Algorithms

Hash algorithms are some of the most popular algorithms used today, especially when looking for a specific ID or key in reference to some dataset. Data retrieved through hashing algorithms is identified by its unique index. Before hashing algorithms were available, such searches were conducted through a combination of binary and sorting search algorithms.

Hashing algorithms help you search a list of items to determine whether a specific value is already present within. Routers also use this algorithm to identify and store IP addresses of devices connected to it. This way, no two devices can be assigned the same IP address on the network.

Dynamic Programming

Dynamic programming algorithms help you solve problems by breaking down the complex concerns into smaller discernable units. Once this is done, each small unit is solved independently of the others, and the solutions stored to memory. Once all the small units are solved, the solutions help you work your way up to the ultimate solution to the complex problem that necessitated the algorithm.

Think about it this way, when you write down 2+2+2+2+2, you know the answer is 10. If you add another +2 at the end, you immediately calculate that the answer is 12. You arrive at 12 so fast because in your memory, you already know the answer to the first set, so you only need to add one set of 2. This is how a dynamic programming algorithm works.

Primality Testing Algorithms

In order to figure out whether some random number is a prime number or not, you can use probabilities or deterministic methods. This algorithm is commonly used in cryptography, especially in encryption and decryption. They are also used in hash tables as hash functions.

Exponentiation by Squaring

Try calculating 232. By default, you must perform 32 calculations involving the number 2. This is too much work. However, through this algorithm, you only need to do this 5 times. This algorithm is also referred to as binary exponentiation.

In binary exponentiation, you can compute large positive integer powers very fast in the format O(log2N). The example we have provided is one of the simplest. Binary exponentiation can also be used to compute square matrices and polynomial powers.

8.

Working with Inheritance

The next thing that we are going to take a look at here is going to be the inheritances.

These are a bit more complex than some of the other stuff in this guidebook, but at this point, you are ready to take it on and really work with something that is more advanced.

You will find that when these inheritances come out, we are going to see some of the beauty that is there with the OOP languages that we talked about before, and we can actually go through and reuse parts of the code that we want to work with.

One of the most important out of all the concepts that come with OOP languages is that of the inheritance.

This idea is going to make it easier for us to define a class based on the terms of another class in our code.

This is useful because it allows us to have an easier way to create and maintain one of the applications that we want to work with.

It is also going to be useful in providing an opportunity for us to reuse the functionality of the code and to get the implementation done faster than ever before.

Any time that we want to go through and create a class, rather than having to go through and write out brand new members of data and members of functions each time that you do it, the programmer is able to designate that the new class is supposed to inherit the members of a class that is already found in the code.

This can make it a lot easier than having to redefine the members and the functions as you go through the code again and again.

The class that we are basing our work on, or the existing class, is going to be known as the base class.

Then the new class that we are trying to create, and the one that will take that information and the data or the functions out of the base class, is going to be known as the derived class.

The idea that we are going to see with the inheritance is that it implements the "is a" relationship.

For example, it can work with the idea of a mammal is an animal; the dog is a mammal; hence dog is an animal as well.

This is going to kind of simplify the process that we are working with here, but still, give us a good idea of what we are working with along the way.

The Access Control of Our Inheritance

The next thing that we need to take a look at is access control and inheritance.

A derived class is able to access all of the parts of the base class that are not private at the time.

This means that the members of the base class that should not be accessible to all of the member functions of the derived classes, are going to be declared as private for the base class when we are doing this as well.

You will notice as we go through this that the derived class is going to be able to inherit all of the base class methods.

There are going to be a few different exceptions that we are able to use with this one based on what results we are hoping to get. Some of the exceptions that we need to remember include:

1.   The friend functions that are found with our base class.

2.   The overloaded operators that are there with our base class.

3.   The destructors, the constructors, and any of the copy constructors that are going to happen with our base class.

We need to make sure that we pay special attention to some of the different parts that show up with our access control.

If some restrictions are found in our base class, then this is going to step in and cause some issues with the inheritance that we are working with as well.

And the child or the derived class is going to notice this along the way.

Type of Inheritances

While we are here, we need to take a closer look at the types of inheritances that we are able to work with.

When we try to derive a class from one of our base classes in the first place, then the base class has the possibility of being inherited through a private, a protected, or a public inheritance.

The type of inheritance that you use is going to be specified through the access-specifier, as we talked about above.

Now, you will find that it is not common for us to work with an inheritance that is private or protected, though it is possible to do this.

Just be aware that there are going to be some issues along the way, and these are not as easy to work with.

The method that we are most likely to work with here will be a public inheritance.

Even though the public option is going to be the most common for us to work with, we need to take a look at some of the rules that are going to happen when we work with the different types of inheritances.

The different rules that we need to remember when we are working with this one include:

The Public Inheritance

When we want to derive a new class from a public base class, the public members that are found in our base, or original class, are going to become public members of the derived class.

And then the protected members that are found in our base class will also become protected members of some of the derived classes that we make out of it as well.

a. Was we could guess here, we are going to find that the private members that are found with our base class are never going to be accessible directly from the derived class.

b. We can access them through here.

c. We just need to do some calls to the protected and the public members of our base class to make this happen.

The Protected Inheritance

The second option that we are able to work with is protected inheritance.

When we want to derive a new class from a base class that is protected, the protected and the public members of the base class are going to end up as protected members of the derived class that we want to work with.

Private Inheritance

The final type of inheritance that we are going to work with is private inheritance.

When we are trying to derive a new class from a private base class, both of the protected and the public members of our base class are going to go over to the derived class, but then these are going to be turned into some of the private members instead.

As we can see, all of these are going to be a bit different from one another.

And this is why we need to be careful about the kind of inheritances that we are going to work with.

If you are in a different type of inheritance, then the members are not always going to work the way that you want.

Double-check what you are in, and make sure that this is set to the right kind so that it actually works the way that you want.

9.

Syntax

S yntax is known as the grammar and spelling of a computer programming language. The computer has its own specific language, and the computer can only perform an action if it is typed in the language that it understands. This language is called Syntax. Syntax of a computer programming is also defined as a set of rules that describes the combinations of computer symbols that are part of any element in a computer language or known to be an appropriately structured document. Syntax programming usually contains strings that are like words; if these strings are properly synthesized, it produces correct and valid sentences. Communication flow may differ because of the difference in programs, however, Syntax remains the communication flow between programmers and their computers. It defines how a program should be written and interpreted, and if the language of a program is not well understood by a programmer, Syntax error is bound to occur.

The Importance of Syntax in Computer Programming

Syntax is simply the use of structured language that the computer can interpret, and when a user fails to use a language that the computer can understand, it can cause errors and the execution of the programming command will be unsuccessful. The Syntax is also referred to as a bridge or a means of communication between your computer and you. The essence of Syntax is to be able to work on the computer effectively without any error.

Furthermore, the quality of Syntax makes a task easier and simpler. It also makes reading or understanding code easier.

What is a Syntax Error?

A Syntax Error may occur when the sequence of characters are not written correctly, or the compiler or interpreter cannot understand the source code, so as to generate a machine code. It may also occur if there is a presence of invalid equation.

Levels of Syntax

Lexical Syntax

Lexical Syntax contains all the basic symbols of the programming language in use. In the computer, a sequence of characters is known as a Lexeme. A Lexical Syntax is, however, a rational language, which consists of grammar rules that defines a set of Lexemes.

Concrete Syntax

Concrete Syntax is a set of rules for writing expressions, programs, and statements and how they should be interpreted. It describes how the elements of language have been displayed and edited. The Concrete Syntax describes how the program looks to the programmer.

Abstract Syntax

Abstract Syntax is defined as the internal representation of specific programs by the simplicity of their grammar. The implementation of a language is known as Abstract Syntax. The Abstract Syntax describes the way the program looks to the evaluator or compiler.

Types of Syntax Programming

There are various Syntax Programming Languages, and they are all distinct from each other.

Prolog Syntax and Semantics are a set of rules that describe how the prolog program should be written and interpreted. A Prolog is a logic and declarative language; hence the programmer has to think about the programs in a different way. Prolog Syntax is one of the first languages to be created, and it is still popular among other languages today. It has been proven useful for things like theorem proving, expert systems, term rewriting, automated planning, and natural language planning.

Perl Syntax borrows Syntax language from other languages like Bourbe Shell, Lisp, Smalltalk. The Perl Syntax is a flexible form of language, which can be edited, or manipulated, in whatever form the programmer wants. The Perl Syntax contains both sequences of declarations and statements, and in Perl language, every statement must end with a semicolon. It is also a case sensitive programming language, and does not allow characters and punctuations like @, $, or %.

PHP Syntax and Semantics form a set of rules that describe how the PHP program can be written and interpreted. The PHP Syntax was developed to follow the C Syntax format, so it can be used in web development.

C Syntax is basically a set of rules that a programmer must bear in mind when writing the C program. The C program consists of elements like header files, main function, and program code. C Syntax is a case sensitive language, so a programmer must follow the rules for the C program to prevent Syntax Error.

All C statements must end with a semicolon, and every C instruction should be written in lower case letters. The C language is represented by numbers in three forms, the integral, real, and complex form.

C++ Syntax is a programming language developed by a Danish computer scientist, Bjarne Stroustrup, to be an extension of the C programming language. C++ Syntax is used in varieties of application domains, which makes it a general-purpose language and a standard by the International Organization for Standardization. Although the C++ inherits most of C's Syntax features, however, it offers efficient hardware access and abstractions compared to other languages.

Java Syntax is the set of rules that describes how the Java program should be written and interpreted. However, Java was derived from both

C and C++ Syntax. Despite these derivations, here are few differences between these languages: in Java, there are no available variables or global functions, but there are data members which are considered as global variables.

JavaScript Syntax is the set of rules that a programmer must bear in mind before writing a JavaScript program or interpreting it. The JavaScript defines two types of values, namely: fixed values called literals, and variable values that are called variables. JavaScript literals are important rules that define how fixed values should be written, and the rules guiding the values are as follow:

- Numbers are to be written with or without decimals.
- Strings are text or words written between a single quote and a double quote.

While JavaScript variables are used to store data values, the var keyword is used by JavaScript to declare variables. The var keyword simply means a variable, and a variable can be changed at any time.

Java derives some of its features from Java Syntax, and also inherits some features from Awk and Perl. Despite having a bit of similarities with Java Syntax, it is a totally different language from JavaScript Syntax. JavaScript is case sensitive, and a programmer must always bear that in mind when constructing a statement.

Python Syntax and Semantics are a set of rules that governs how the Python Program will be written and interpreted. The Python Program was developed with a high level of readability, and it uses English keywords more and even frequently, than other languages. Moreover, the Python language has a few similarities to Perl, C, and Java Syntax, and also some distinct differences between these languages. A Python program is, however, divided into a logical line that is created from one or two physical lines. When this logical line is terminated, it is usually done by the to-ken newline.

A line in computer programming contains just tabs, spaces, and possibly a comment called a black line, which is usually ignored by the python's interpreter. While a physical line, on the other hand, are sets of sequence of characters that are terminated at the end-of-life sequence. The Python Syntax uses words known as reserved words, and these words are as follow: false, class, finally, none, continue, for, from, global, as, assert, break, etcetera.

Lua Syntax, is a high-level multi-paradigm that contains a lot of instructions that was created for a specific use and execution of a task. The Lua program allows programmers to implement namespaces, classes, and other features. Lua is simple and flexible; Haskell Syntax is a multi-dimensional language, and here the few reasons why it is so. Haskell Syntax is a language that is suitable for any kind of program, which is why Haskell Syntax is addressed as a general-purpose language.

Aside from its ability to fit into any program, it is also a statically typed language. The Haskell program is divided into two phases, the compile time and the run time. When each of your variables has a type that indicates the kind of data that variable is allowed to hold, it is a compiled time phase. Java and C Syntax are examples of a statically typed language.

In addition, Haskell can allow you to create anonymous functions, get them stored in variables, and pass them to other functions as an argument. The functions of the Haskell language will always produce the same result and value.

Syntax in SQL

I believe by now, you already have an overview of what Syntax is all about. Syntax is simply sticking to grammar and rules guiding the programming languages. Every language has its own Syntax, likewise SQL. Every punctuation, symbols, characters has a meaning when used in SQL. Every command in SQL must end with a semicolon. When writing a command, whether while using SQL or another programming language, it is effective that you learn and do things according to the rules. Leaving too much space, using a capital letter can cause Syntax Error, if it is the punctuations or letters used wrongly.

Preventing Syntax Error is possible if you always create a clean and concise programming command.

10.

Creating Your First Database

B efore having a successful database with practical tables in SQL programming, both the creation of a database and then a table is required. However, there are several SQL data application software out there, but all have almost a similar step of creating a new database and tables. When you create your first database system, you will then have to design a table where you will feed your data and store it more securely and effectively. SQL offers a free graphical user interface, and it is easy to create. The following is a step by step guide on how to create your first SQL database and tables before thinking of feeding your data.

Steps

Step 1: SQL Server Management Studio Software Installation

The firsts step in creating your first database and table is by acquiring the SQL software available for free online from Microsoft. This software comes fully packed, allowing you to interact and manage the SQL server with limited command-line instructions. Besides, it is crucial when it comes to using databases when in remote regions. Mac users can, however, utilize open-source programs, for instance, SQuirrel SQL, to maneuver through the Database system.

Step 2: Launch the SQL Studio

When you launch the SQL studio, the software occasionally requests for a server at first that you will prefer using all along or the one you are using presently. If you have an already existing one, you may choose to input the permissions, authenticate, and connect. Some may prefer local database systems by setting a new name authenticate using a preferred name or address. Launching the SQL server management studio begins the process of interacting with the software and a path to creating your first database and table.

Step 3: Identify Database Folder

Immediately after the connection is made on either the local or remote, a window will open on the left of the screen. On top, there will be a server where it will connect to. If not, you may click on the icon '+,' which will display multiple elements, including the option to create a new database. In some versions, you may see the icon for creating a new database immediately on the left drop-down window. You can then click on 'Create New Database.'

Step 4: Create a New Database

As mentioned in step 3, the drop-down menu will fully display multiple options, including the one to create a new database. First, you will configure the database according to your parameters as well as providing the name for ease of identification. Most users prefer leaving the settings in their default, but you can change them if you are familiar with how they impact your process of data storage in the system. Note that when you create the database name, two files will generate the data automatically and log files. Data files are responsible for the storage of data while log files track all the changes, modifications, and other alterations made in the database.

Step 5: Create Your Tables

Databases often do not store data unless structures in forms of rows and tables are created for that data to remain organized. Tables are the primary storage units where data is held, but initially, you have to create the table before you insert the information. Similar to creating a new database, tables are also straightforward when creating. In the Databases folder, expand the window then right-click on Tables and choose 'Nee Table.' Windows will open, displaying a table that can be easily manipulated towards the number of rows and columns, titles, and how you want to organize your work. In this step, you will succeed in creating both the database and table, therefore, moving forward in organizing your task.

Step 6: Developing the Primary Key

The primary key plays a significant role in databases as it acts as a record number or ID for easy identification and remembrance when you view the page later. As such, it highly recommended creating these keys in the first column. There are many ways to do this and include entering the ID in the column field by typing 'int' and deselecting the 'Allow

Nulls.' Select the key icon found in the toolbar and marks it as the Primary key.

Step 7: Structure the Tables

Tables typically have multiple columns, also referred to as fields, and each column represents one element of data entries. When creating your table, you initially structured it to fit the number of data entries, therefore essential for each dataset as other primary keys. Thus, the structuring process will entail identifying each column with a given set of data. For example, First name column, Last name, and address column, among others.

Step 8: Creating Other Columns

Immediately you create the columns for primary keys; you will notice that there appear more columns below it. These are not for primary keys but essential for the insertion of other information. As such, ensure you input the correct data for each column to avoid filling the table with the wrong information. In the column, you will enter the 'nchar,' which is a data type for text, 'int' used for whole numbers, and 'decimal' for storage of decimal numbers.

Step 9: Saving the Table

After you finish creating the content in each field, you will notice that your table will consist of rows and columns. However, you will need to first save the table before entering the information. This can be done by selecting the Save icon also in the toolbar and name your table. When naming your table, ensure that you create a name that you can easily relate to the content or recognize. Besides, databases with different tables should have different names so that they can be identified easily.

Step 10: Add Data

Once the table is saved, you can now add the data into the system feeding each field with relevant information. However, you can confirm if the table is saved by expanding the Tables Folder and try to see if our table name is listed. If not, use the Table Folder to refresh the tables, and you will see your table. Back in the table, Right-click on the table where a drop dialog box will appear and select 'Edit Top 200 Rows'. The Window will then display fields for you to add data but ignore the primary keys as they will fill automatically. Continue with the same process until when you enter the last data in the table.

Step 11: Running the Table

After you have finished working on the table, you have to save the content so that you do not lose your work. As the table is already saved, click on 'Execute SQL' on the toolbar when you have finished entering data, and it will execute the process of feeding each data you entered into the columns. The parsing process may take a few seconds, depending on a load of data. If there are any errors in the feeding process, the system will show you where you input data incorrectly. More so, you can execute the program parsing of all the data by using the combination of 'ctrl' and 'R.'

Step 12: Data Querying

At this step, you have created your first database and table and successfully saved the information through SQL language programming. The database is now fully functional, and you henceforth create more tables within a single database. However, there is a limit on how many tables per database, but many users do not worry about this rule. You can, therefore, create new database systems you want and create more tables. At this end, you can query your data for reports or any relevant purposes, such as organizational or administrative purposes. Often, having a general idea of SQL programming, especially for putting it into practice in creating databases and tables, allows you to advance your learning skills.

Creating Your First Database and Table Using Command Line

You use SQL commands and statements to create databases and tables. The same applies to SQL Server Management Studio like the above guide, but commands and statements are used to give instructions to the system to perform a given function. As to build your first database, you use the command' SELECT DATABASE (database_name)' and hitting the execute button to create the program. The message on the screen should, therefore, be 'Command(s) completed successfully,' showing that your database has been created.

As to use the database, run the command 'USE (database_name),' which tells the query window to run the new database program. On the other hand, creating a new table entails running the command 'CREATE TABLE (table_name).' Entering data follows the command 'INSERT DATA INTO (table_name), VALUES (table_name),' and repeating the same process for all the datasets you have. The same also allows for viewing the data you saved and includes the command format 'SELECT * FROM (table_name). ' All the above commands are the critical ones when it comes to maneuvering through different SQL databases. As such, it is always essential to learn about each SQL basic commands to execute programs readily.

11.

Working with Popular Apps

Machines have different applications that run independently or dependent on other programs without damaging other programs in the system unless triggered. When you open one app, for instance, it tends to perform its essential functions with limited hindrance to other programs already running. This phase will then discuss popular applications used as programming language tools, especially in database management systems. You should note that computer applications come from different developers, with some designing more than one, such as significant companies like Microsoft. Therefore, using various computer programs tend to differ more so on functionality and design.

Using SQLite

Unlike other database management systems, SQLite is a relational database system (RDBMS) but not a client-server database. The software program was developed by Richard Hipp and first released in August 2000. SQLite is crucial as an embedded database application essential as a storage application for both client and local on platforms such as web browsers. As such, it is mostly used in database engines as it readily binds to different programming languages. It is, therefore, crucial for operating systems, embedded systems, and web browsers.

When compared to other databases such as MySQL, Oracle, and SQL Servers, SQLite functions differently as it may purpose is to solve a unique problem when it comes to local data storage for individual use. In this case, SQLite is suitable for the internet of things and embedded gadgets such as smartphones as it lacks an administrative function as well as thriving in network edges. As already mentioned, SQLite is also essential in websites for medium and low traffic sites on database usage. It is also applicable in file formatting as an on-disk and data analysis for more massive datasets by use of the SQLite3 command-line shell. Other applications include caching of enterprise data, informational transfer, archiving files, ad hoc replacement, and as a training tool for educational purposes.

Using Apache OpenOffice Base

Apache OpenOffice is another database system and a successor of OpenOffice.org consisting of a word processor, spreadsheet, presentation software, drawing application, database management software, and formula editor. Apache OpenOffice can write different file formats, including Microsoft office, while being compatible with Linux, Windows, and macOS. It is a product of the Apache Software Foundation initially released in May 2018. Besides, it is an open office productivity software and easy to use as it incorporates all other file formats, used immediately on the acquisition, and supported by thousands of enthusiasts.

Using PostgreSQL

Also known as Postgre, PostgreSQL is another free and open-source RDBMS designed to handle significant workloads from individual computers commercial use. It focuses on extensibility, and technical standards primarily create for Mac users. However, versions of Linux, Windows, and other operating systems are available. PostgreSQL was first introduced in the market in July 1996, developed by PostgreSQL Global Development Group. As a database management system, this software allows for the isolation of transactions as well as the atomicity and consistency of data handling. Development began in 1982 with the current modifications allowing for user-friendly interfaces suitable for the addition of custom functions essential for programming languages such a Python, JavaScript, and C/C+.

Using Adobe ColdFusion

First released in 1995, ColdFusion is commercial use software primarily for web application development. It was created by J. J. Allaire and enhanced by Adobe Systems Incorporated as a programming language to link HTML pages to databases and included IDE in 1996. Using Adobe ColdFusion allows you to experience a new system full of unique features to handle different types of data. It accompanies an expressive and powerful function making the creation and designing of modern web application software much higher when compared to other programming languages. As a database management system, Adobe ColdFusion allows users to access simplified databases accompanied by other benefits such as client/server management, code generation, and operational graphics, among others.

Using PHP

PHP (Hypertext Preprocessor) is a multipurpose scripting computer language designed by Rasmus Lerdorf in 1994 and released in 1995. It was previously referred to as Personal Home Pages used to develop Static and Dynamic websites as well as web applications. The scripts created and designed by PHP can only be read and interpreted by servers that have a PHP program installed. Using PHP is one of the ways to learn how to code values, which results in the development of newer versions of web applications. PHP ran on web servers, command lines, client-side graphical user interface, and supported on various web hosting platforms. The way it enables users to operate readily, build, customize, and have an extension of their own when working with PHP.

Using IBM Db2

Db2 is a group of database products such as servers developed by IBM and was first released in 1993. It is compatible with Linux, Windows, and UNIX operating systems written in C/C+, Java, and assembly computer languages. It supports different functions, which include object-relational and non-relational features such as XML. When compared to SQL, Db2 also accompanies tables but includes objects, for instance, indexes significant data containers, for example, table's spades. While SQL is a standard computer programming tool that focuses on data tables accessed in a relational database; Db2 family consists of databases, warehouses, BigSQL, event store, and cloud-oriented objects such as warehouse on the cloud. The use of IBM Db2 allows for data storage, analysis, and immediate retrieval when the need arises as it fit with oriented features crucial for system functionality.

Using Oracle Express

Oracle Express is a web-based software that runs on Oracle database systems developed by Oracle Corporation with the first release in 2004. It supports different operating systems such as Linux, Oracle Scolaris, and HP-UX essential for the creation of complex web applications used in modern web browsers. The Oracle Express application includes the system menu commands and database home pages, which help in the production of environments that facilitates its functions. System menu commands allow users to access the original features of the database, while home pages are crucial for performing different database administrative functions. Some of the functions include monitoring of database storage and sessions and initialization parameters. The use of Oracle Express allows a user to, therefore, run values which help in computer languages crucial for modern web browsers.

Using MariaDB

MariaDB is a form of MySQL relational database management system as well free and open-source application. Released in October 2009, MariaDB was designed to be highly compatible with the MySQL database. However, the compatibility has risen to become a drop-in replacement of the use of MySQL over time. In comparison, however, MariaDB is quite faster and secure with recent updates of up to two times when compared to MySQL. More so, you can integrate data from MariaDB while using one node timely with other database systems. MariaDB can again connect to the different databases but take various processes depending on the operating system.

Using MySQL

MySQL is another open-source RDBMS and cofounded by Michael Widenius utilizing the concept of SQL programming. MySQL is used in different popular websites such as Facebook, YouTube, and Flickr as well as database-driven web programs such as phpBB, WordPress, and Drupal, among others. The initial release was made in May 1995, written in C and C++ language with modifications made on its vast range of features. As to use the MySQL database, you initially have to install the application with the required configurations, run and launch the program. Subsequently, you can connect to the MySQL database using different steps, depending on the operating system.

Using Microsoft Access

Microsoft Access was developed, designed, and modified by Microsoft and was first released in November 1992. With its ability to link and access data stored in other programs and databases, the application has gained popularity and used mostly for individual use. It has also helped software developers and engineers, data architectures, and power users to create other programs. Microsoft access remains supported by Visual Basic for Applications, and ActiveX Data Objects, making it used in the form of reports.

Using Microsoft SQL Server

Microsoft has also incorporated Microsoft SQL Server, which is another relational database management system used as a software product for the storage and retrieval of data when requested by software applications. Different audiences use the software on both small-scale and large internet facing programs, including other concurrent users. Microsoft SQL Server was first released in April 1989 with currently available in different editions to suit various needs such as web, enterprise, express, and business intelligence. There exist also special editions, which include azure, fast track, compact (SQL CE) and analytics platform system, and discontinuous editions such as MSDE, personal edition, and datacenter. As a user, Microsoft SQL Servers are essential for the organization of data in a systematic manner, therefore, allowing for data retrieval efficiently.

Using Microsoft ASP

Microsoft ASP (Active Server Pages) is a computer language released by Microsoft used for dynamic websites though older and often used in the 1990s. It was used in Windows 95 and 98 and a scripting computer programming language allowing for simple coding included in HTML and run in servers. The file extension of ASP is .asp, and the program is often sent to the browser, though it can be changed. Besides, Microsoft ASP allows other computer languages to be used in the script and include Jscript. Despite being an older database management system, ASP enables simplicity on usage as lines of the coding program can be quickly added in an online form included as URL. Therefore, APS becomes more interactive and results achieved without advanced programming skills. Unlike other database programming software, Microsoft ASP allows for the extension of functionalities. This way, it has resulted in more effective results making it be remaining in use today among the modern versions.

Using Microsoft ASP.NET

ASP.NET is a modern Microsoft ASP format that accompanies an open-source and web application servers essential for web development for designing dynamic web pages. The application was incorporated in January 2002, allowing programmers to enjoy modern ASP features to build dynamic websites, programs, and applications. Unlike ASP, ASP.NET is more applicable in supporting several programming models such as ASP.NET web forms, MVC, web API, signalR, and web pages. Microsoft and other companies have created the tools used in ASP.NET for the benefit of retuning productive outcomes. The application is free for download for all users, which is then installed and launched to enable you to execute programs readily.

Using Microsoft Query

Database management software from Microsoft is a query that enables users to acquire visuals methods essential for database querying by use of text string examples, file names, and document lists, as it features the query by example tools, the application works by enabling the system to convert inputs into formal database queries by use of SQL. As such, users can readily engage in powerful searches as a form of data retrieval without skills developing skills or experience in SQL. Microsoft Query uses the Query-by-Example, feature created NY Moshe M. Zloof in the 1970s. More so, it also adopts the Microsoft Access user-friendly interface allowing learners to readily learn and understand relational database management systems to use in small businesses. Microsoft Query application is also used in access as an embedded tool in a spreadsheet.

12.

Exception Handling

What Is a Bug?

Bugs must be the most hated creatures a programmer can have. A bug in the programmer's eyes is a bug in a program. These bugs can cause errors or unintended consequences. Many times, a bug can be fixed after the fact. There are, of course, irremediable lessons. The European Ariane 5 rocket exploded within a minute of its first launch. An after-action investigation revealed that a floating-point number in the navigator was to be converted to an integer, but the value was too large to overflow. In addition, a British helicopter crashed in 1994, killing 29 people. The investigation revealed that the helicopter's software system was "full of flaws." In the 2001 movie: "A Space Odyssey," the supercomputer HAL kills almost all of the astronauts because of two goals in its program conflict.

In English, bug means defect. Engineers have long used the term bug to refer to mechanical defects. And there's a little story about using the word bug in software development. A moth once flew into an early computer and caused a computer error. Since then, bugs have been used to refer to bugs. The moth was later posted in a journal and is still on display at the National Museum of American History.

Code:

```
for result in range(5)

print(result)
```

Python does not run this program. It will alert you to grammatical errors:

Output is:

SyntaxError: invalid Syntax

There are no Syntax errors in the following program, but when Python is run, you will find that the subscript of the reference is outside the scope of the list element.

```
result= [12, 24, 36]

print(result[4])
```

The program aborts the error reporting

Output:

IndexError: list index out of range

The above type of Error that the compiler finds only at Runtime is called the Runtime Error. Because Python is a dynamic language, many operations must be performed at run time, such as determining the type of a variable. As a result, Python is more prone to run-time errors than a static language.

There is also a type of Error called a Semantic Error. The compiler thinks that your program is fine and can run normally. But when you examine the program, it turns out that it's not what you want to do. In general, such errors are the most insidious and the most difficult to correct. For example, here's a program that prints the first element of a list.

```
mix = ["first", "second", "third"]

print(mix[1])
```

There is no error in the program, normal print. But what you find is that you print out the second element, B, instead of the first element. This is because the Python list starts with a subscript from 0, so to refer to the first element, the subscript should be 0, not 1.

Debugging

The process of fixing a bug in a program is called debugging. Computer programs are deterministic, so there is always a source of error. Of course, sometimes spending a lot of time not being able to debug a program does create a strong sense of frustration, or even a feeling that you are not suitable for program development. Others slam the keyboard and think the computer is playing with itself. From my personal observation, even the best programmers will have bugs when they write programs. It's just that good programmers are more at peace with debugging and don't doubt themselves about bugs. They may even use the debug process as a kind of training, to work with their computer knowledge by better understanding the root cause of the error.

Actually, debugging is a bit like being a detective. Collect the evidence, eliminate the suspects, and leave the real killer behind. There are many ways to collect evidence, and many tools are available. For starters, you don't need to spend much time with these tools. By inserting a simple print() function inside the program, you can see the state of the variable and how far it has run. Sometimes, you can test your hypothesis by replacing one instruction with another and seeing how the program results change. When all other possibilities are ruled out, what remains is the true cause of the error.

On the other hand, debug is also a natural part of writing programs. One way to develop a program is Test-Driven Development (TDD). For Python to be such a convenient, dynamic language, it's a good place to start by writing a small program that performs a specific function. Then, on the basis of the small program, gradually modify, so that the program continues to evolve, and finally, meet the complex requirements. Throughout the process, you keep adding features, and you keep fixing mistakes. The important thing is, you've been coding. The Python author himself loves this kind of programming. So, debug is actually a necessary procedure for you to write the perfect program.

Exception Handling in Detail

For errors that may occur at run time, we can deal with them in the program in advance. This has two possible purposes: one is to allow the program to perform more operations before aborting, such as providing more information about the error. The other is to keep the program running after it makes a mistake.

Exception handling can also improve program fault tolerance. The following procedure uses the exception handling:

The program that requires exception handling is wrapped in a try structure. Except explains how the program should respond when a particular error occurs. Program, input() is a built-in function to receive command-line input. The float() function is used to convert other types of data to floating-point numbers. If you enter a string, such as "P," it will not be converted to a floating-point number, and trigger ValueError, and the corresponding except will run the program that belongs to it. If you enter 0, then dividing by 0 will trigger ZeroDivisionError. Both errors are handled by the default program, so the program does not abort.

The complete Syntax for exception handling is:

try:

... (code should be written here)

```
except  exception1:

... ( code should be written here)

except exception2:

... ( code should be written here)

else:

... ( code should be written here)

finally:

...
```

If an exception occurs within a try, the exception is assigned, and except is executed. Exception layer by layer to see if it is exception1, exception2, and so on, until it is found to belong to, execute the corresponding statements in except. If there is no exception in try, so the except part skips the execution of the else statement. Finally is something you do in the end, whether or not there is an exception. If except is followed by no parameters, then all exceptions will be handled by the program.

13.

Gathering Your Data

The first thing that we need to take a look at is how to gather up the data that we need to accomplish this kind of process in data science. We need to have a chance to go through and look at our data, figure out what kind of data is out there that we can use, and so much more. But figuring out where to get that data, how much to collect, and what kind is going to be right to help us figure out more about our customers and industry, can be hard.

There is an overabundance of options out there when it comes to the kind of data that we want to use along the way. We need to make sure that we are picking out the right kinds of data, rather than just collecting data because it is there and looks like the right thing to work with. When we are able to organize this in the manner that we need, and we make sure that we actually get the good data, even if it is not organized and structured the way that we want in the beginning, it is going to be so important.

That is why we are going to spend some time in this phase exploring what we are able to do with our data, how it is going to work for our needs and even some of the places where you can look in order to find the data that you would like to work with. With that in mind, we need to dive right in!

Know Your Biggest Business Problem

There is a lot of data out there, and it is not going to take long doing some searching before you find that you will end up in a rabbit hole with all of this information if you don't have a plan or a direction for what you are going to do with all of that information. There is a ton of good data, but if you just let it lead you rather than having a clear path in front of you, you are going to end up with a lot of problems and will never get the decision making help that you need.

If you have already gathered up your data, then this point is gone and we just need to work from there. You can form through your biggest business problem, the one that you would like to spend your time focusing on and fixing, and then sort through the data there and see what changes you are able to make, and what data out of that large source you have is going to make the biggest difference. Don't be scared to just leave some of the data for later, and don't let the fact that you may not use some of the data hold you back either.

During this time, we want to focus on knowing the best information, this is going to be the best way to make sure that you get the information needed to really propel your business into the future. Even some of the information is left behind, that is fine. You may come back to it later if you need some of it. But only the best data that you have should be used for your algorithms to give you the best results.

Now, if you have not had the time to go and collect any data yet, this is something we can work with as well. Forming the problem that you would like to solve, and having a clear path can help you to sort through all of the noise that is out there, and will ensure that you are really able to get things done in the process. You need to make sure that you are searching in the right places, and looking for the information that is going to be the most critical for what you are trying to accomplish, the part that is going to be so important when it is time to handle some of the work that is out there.

Places to Look for the Data

The next thing that we need to consider when it comes to this process of gathering up the data and using it in the manner that we would like, is figuring out where to find and look for the data that we need. There are actually so many different places where we are able to look for the data that we want to handle, but this is part of the beauty of the modern system that we are using today.

We have to remember, though, that most of the data that we will collect today is not going to be organized or structured. We will look at some of the steps that you are able to take in order to organize the data a little bit later, so this is not a big deal. Just be prepared that you will have to go through and take on a few extra steps in order to make sure that your data stays organized in the manner that you would like, and that it is not going to be as nice and neat as you would like in the long run.

So, the places where you are able to look for some of the data that you would like to use in this process will be varied, and it often depends on what you are hoping to get out of this process. You want to concentrate on getting the highest-quality data in the process that you can, though. This is going to ensure that you are going to be able to find the data that you need and that the algorithms you use later on will really be able to provide you with some of the best results and insights that you need to move your business forward.

There are still a lot of places where you are able to look to find the data that you want. You will find that you can pick out data from websites (especially if you would like to work with web scraping), from social media sites if you are using one from surveys and focus groups of your own, and from other companies who may have collected the information and are using it to help out others along the way.

You may find that if you are able to bring up data from a more unique source as well, this is going to get you even further ahead with some of the work that you want to do. It will ensure that you will have data that no one else is going to have, and will provide you with some new patterns and insights, as long as you make sure that the data is high quality and will actually be good for your needs.

Where to Store the Data?

We also need to consider where we would like to store some of the data that we are working with along the way. You are likely to gather up a lot of data in the process, and it isn't likely that you just want to have it sitting around without a purpose or having it in a safe and secure location. This is especially true if you are working with data that is your own, data you got from surveys and other places that you don't want others getting ahold of.

There are a number of different places where you are able to store this data for your own needs, and the location that you choose is often going to depend on what works for you. If you have enough storage space on your own network, this can be a great place to start. Then the data is always safe and secure with you and easy to reach. You just need to make sure that you are keeping some good security measures on your system, so you don't end up losing that information and no longer having it at your disposal.

Many companies decide to put it on a web-based storage area, like the cloud. This adds in another level of protection to the information and will ensure that you are able to reach that data when you need it as well. There are a lot of these kinds of storage areas that we can work with, and you will find that you are able to get this to work for some of your needs pretty well. Whether your storage needs are large or not, you will find that storing this data is going to make a world of difference when it is time to handle this process, and you just have to decide how much you would like to use ahead of time.

Knowing where to find the data that you need to start out with your data analysis and data science project is going to be super important.

This is going to set the tone for the work that you are able to do later on and how much success you are going to have with your project as well. Make sure to search around for the data that is going to be needed in this, and pay attention to how much of it you will need, where you are likely to find it, and more.

Conclusion

This is the end of the guidebook. The next milestone is to make the best use of your new-found wisdom of Basic Programming, Data Science, Data Analysis, and Machine Learning that have resulted in the birth of the powerhouse, which is the "Silicon Valley." So many companies, that span a lot of different industries, are able to benefit when they work with data analysis. This allows them to get a lot of the power and control that they want for their respective industries and will ensure that they will be able to really impress their customers and get some good results in the process. Learning how to use a data analysis is going to change the game in how you do business, as long as it is used in the proper manner.

As a beginner to programming, we want to congratulate you on making it through the first Procedures of this wonderful journey. Now, with your feet past the threshold, we invite you to take a look at the world beyond and really let your imagination go wild. There is no limit to what you can do once you've put your mind to it.

You have been given the basics of programming. You have suffered through a multitude of Syntax errors, exceptions, and potential system crashes. And now your eyes have been opened to the world of programming. So, where do you go from here?

The answer is simple: Go wherever the wind takes you.

At this point, you should know what it is that you want to do with your newly acquired programming skills. As the magician that you are now, you have to forge your own path and decide how to best utilize your magic. For instance, most of the program authors' work involves using Application Program Interfaces (APIs). This means that the need to gather and process data is never-ending.

When it comes to yourself, there is nothing that can be better offered than information about what is out there for you to explore. There are many disciplines that are in need of your programming abilities. These few may help you choose which way you need to go.

Data scientists are in need of program developers, as it is an extremely good tool that offers many modules to solve a lot of limitations found in other languages. However, the most important thing is how well Program developers are paid.

Machine Learning is best practiced in Programming, although there are other programming languages that have libraries to support it. None come close to Python, though. It is being used by corporations like Google, along with thousands of programmers around the world.

Web development using Python and Django makes it very easy to build web applications. If your passion lies there, you can do in mere minutes what it would take other developers to do in hours.

Whatever your choice, wherever the journey may take you from here, just know that you are ready to take on all the challenges you may face.

We truly believe that you are armed with some of the best informational bullets we can give you, and enough tips and tricks to get you started in this world of codes. As with everything else in life, view this as an adventure, and don't be afraid to venture forth and explore new territories. There is still so much more program that can offer, and for the programmer in you looking for more advanced techniques and tips, just explore the world of programming. The more you do, the more you'll learn, and the more you'll want to learn.

I hope you have learned something!

CODING

FOR KIDS

The Complete and Intuitive Guide to Learn

How to Code for Beginners

SEAN DAMON

Table of Contents

Introduction 116

Chapter 1: What Is Coding 120

Chapter 2: Programming Languages And Ides 126

Chapter 3: Debugging 133

Chapter 4: Loops 140

Chapter 5: What Programming Language Should You Learn? 147

Chapter 6: Pre-Schoolers Offline Coding 154

Chapter 7: Working With Files 162

Chapter 8: Conditionals 177

Chapter 9: Oop (Object-Oriented Programming) 186

Chapter 10: Preparing Your Self For Coding 195

Chapter 11: The Future Of Machine Learning 201

Conclusion 205

Introduction

C oding is a good and useful skill that every child should learn. In later years, this skill may be used to create and develop great things. These things may be intended for entertainment during the childhood and teenage years. But, many of these things raise an interest in programming that can later be a solid basis for a career in computer science, engineering, or some other computer-related profession. These professions today are very popular among young people.

There are so many different programming languages, intended for creating different sorts of programs. The general rule is that any language can be used to make any kind of program. But, is it true? We will discover the answer to this question in this book. Some of these programming languages can be hard to learn, while others are as simple as the alphabet we learned as small children. Just keep in mind that every person (and this applies to children also) is an individual. Consider allowing them input when it comes to deciding which of the programming languages they like best. You should present them with a few, for example, Ruby, Python, and Java, explain to them the advantages and disadvantages are for each of them. Then, to keep it interesting, you might give them examples of programs and platforms they are familiar with and explain to them which programming language they are based on. For example, if you tell a child who has an account on Twitter that this social network was built using the Ruby programming language, they may become interested in learning more about Ruby, because this language is what made their favorite pastime possible. By learning about the programming languages that made their favorite games, applications, and social networks possible, they will also learn how to behave safely when it comes to computers and data they post on the Internet. So, this is another good thing that will come out of the first coding course.

Some program languages are very simple, like Python. This language looks more like a normal speech than like a programming language in the common sense of the word. That is why this program is very easy to learn and easy to use. It suits beginners best, but more experienced programmers can use it too. Let's examine why it is so easy to use. Coding is simple, although it may not look that way. That, in fact, is a common misconception about coding in any language, including Python. If you know how to give detailed instructions on how to do something (writing and sending an email to another person, for example), then you can learn how to code using the Python programming language. It's as simple as that.

When Installing Program is generally so easy, and in this day and age, many operating systems (Linux and UNIX for example) come with Program already installed as an integral part of the operating system, even some of the Windows computers (especially those manufactured by HP) now let us come with Program that already installed. When it comes to learning how Program works, how to use it, and what it can do for us, you have a variety of sources to choose from. You can learn it all by yourself, reading books, or using help available on the Internet. These could include online courses, eBooks and even blogs written by experienced programmers who wanted to make things easier for you as a beginner. When starting out, it's wise to take a look at freely available online information. Furthermore, there are countless online tutorials available to move on to after reading this book, and many of these tutorials are cost-free and intended specifically for beginners. Nearly every program developer that has any level of success in creating programs tends to share their success with the rest of the world. This is done mostly through blogging and videos and tutorials posted on YouTube. You can follow their blogs, or watch the instructional videos they post on YouTube. That way, you can easily learn the basics of any programming language and its syntax, because, these people post very detailed videos/texts, explaining every single aspect to the core. There are also options to chat with them. That way, you can ask them for an explanation of Python's syntax if that is what you are interested in. If you are working on a Python-based program or project, and you encounter difficulties using it, you may ask some of these bloggers for advice or help in solving your problem.

Another way of learning about Python and how it works is the search on an Internet library with copious amounts of Python tutorials. This library or database is called the "ActiveState Python Cookbook." This is a certified tutorial book collection available on the official Python website. There are many instructional tools available (including videos for visual learners) there which can be useful to you and the children in your life, and can easily be paired with the other resources mentioned earlier in this phase to create a solid basis for getting started with coding in Python. In the end, the choice of learning method is entirely up to you. Use the one that you feel it's the best for you or your students.

One important thing you should know about using Python is that it is free. You are not required to pay any kind of fee to use it. Python is a part of the so-called "open source concept." This is a concept that has one goal: to bring programs to you as end-users, without demanding a charge for it. If you download something that is "open source," this is completely free. This allows us to use the latest programming innovations to our advantage and for our benefit. In practice, the choice of the programming language is often dictated by other real-world factors. I have mentioned the so-called "YouTubers" posting their video tutorials before. These people show you how one programming language works by giving you instructions using a simple example for nearly every field covered by a given programming language. If you are a visual type when it comes to learning, then this is ideal for you. They show you every step that needs to be taken and also explain the meaning of every word/symbol used for writing code. You might want to explore what these examples are and give them a try yourself. That way, you (or your students) can learn from practical experience how to make programs, not just in Python, but in any other computer programming language. Use the source code on your system freely.

CHAPTER 2:

What Is Coding

Some people say coding is hard; some say it is easy. It's all subjective. However, coding can be a bit complicated, especially when you are starting from Scratch. So you need to understand how code works. Exactly what happens when you code? Do you know the mechanics behind coding? That's the reason for this introduction.

Coding/writing computer programs are not new. It's been around for quite some time, about 50 years ago. Bill Gates, the world's richest man, wrote codes for fun on his IBM, before a lot of us where born or even dreamt about codes. At the moment, coding is a favorite pastime of many, just the same way that the skill has enabled some people to be able to do very cool and useful things and earn a lot of money doing them.

Coding runs the world today as we know it. Although a lot of people don't know this, there's coding embedded into virtually all the gadgets we use today. From your television sets to air conditioners, microwaves, phones, projectors, and many more items, all these have been programmed to do something. This is not just limited to electronic gadgets; even mechanical devices like your car also have some programming in it too. How about our websites and even machinery for manufacturing and farming? What coding can do or where it is used is almost inexhaustible. But surprisingly, not many people know about this. They only believe coding to be for website development and perhaps for building mobile apps.

There are different kinds of coding or programming languages, and they are used to achieve different things. Some are more versatile or will serve as a background like HTML and C (although a lot of people will argue that HTML is not a programming language, we'll get to that later). Others are a little bit more specific, like Ruby and JavaScript.

For the uninitiated, what is coding? How can you define it? Are coding and programming the same thing? Well, let's dive into the nitty-gritty of this book.

Coding can be defined as the act of telling the computer what to do in a language that it can understand. The languages used to achieve this are called programming languages. And they include Python, JavaScript, C, C++, and many more.

If your code is right, the computer will perform a certain desired action or actions, will behave a certain way.

Computers don't understand human languages. Yeah, I know that you're reading this probably on a computer and thinking to yourself how you've clicked on icons written in the English language, and the computer has performed a desirable action. This is only possible because someone has programmed your computer's operating systems to be able to take in software which you can then use for whatever you want to use it. So behind your operating system, whether you use Windows, Mac, or Linux, a lot of coding has gone into it. Try using a computer without an OS and see if you can do anything with it.

So the language of computers is what we call machine language, it is in binary 1 and 0. Now, what a certain programming language does is to act as some sort of translator or interpreter between human language and binary. I mean there's no way your computer is speaking "human," and there's no way you're speaking binary, just 1 and 0. Imagine you just talking in 1 and 0, weird, right? But that's the only language your computer understands. So you write in code, that's actually some sort of human language, then another program changes it into the computer's language. Then your computer can understand and do what you have told it to do. This is a much more complicated process, but then I'm sure you get the big picture of how coding works. A document full of these codes is called a script. Each script or a line of code is supposed to make the computer behave in a certain way when properly written. One script might be to make retweet someone's tweet, another might be to block someone on twitter, and the list is endless of what code can do.

Programming vs. Coding

We often hear such phrases such as, "I'm learning to code," "My boyfriend is a programmer," "I'm learning to code websites," or "I can program very well with JavaScript." The fact is that these two words— coding and programming—have been used interchangeably and will continue that way for a long time. Now the question is, are they actually the same thing, the exact same thing?

What is Programming?

We've defined the coding, right? Okay, so a definition of programming will give us an idea of what it is and what it is not. Let's use a very simple analogy. You have a digital phone, and I can assume that you set the alarm. You perhaps set the alarm to ring at the same time every day except on weekends.

Maybe you muted a particular word on your Twitter so that anytime that word is mentioned, you don't see it.

Basically, this is what you did. You said to your devices if this happens, you do this. When its 5 am Mondays to Fridays, the alarm rings, once this particular number calls, block it. Once this word is mentioned, mute, I don't want to see it.

You see. It could be said that you programmed your device to behave in certain ways in certain situations. There were already instructions available from the manufacturer of the device; all you did was just tell your phone to obey the instructions in certain situations.

Programming could be said to be providing instructions for something or someone to follow. For example, soldiers at the sound of certain commands will perform certain manoeuvres. It could be to march, charge, and withdraw, etc. Therefore, programming deals with the creation of a way (a program) that provides executable instructions for a machine to carry out, making it behave in a certain way.

So the process of creating those instructions which your phone followed is coding, and then making your device do what those instructions have said is programming.

A programmer is more like an engineer. A client wants a car that can fly. The engineer designs it, and then a technologist builds it based on the design the engineer has provided.

So coding is about writing codes, while a programmer does many other things. These include problem-solving, planning, conceptualization, leadership, critical thinking, understanding data structures, implementing algorithms, and many more. A programmer looks for the best way a project (be it an app, a website, or something else) can be done the fastest and easier way. He breaks them down into bite-sized chunks, and then it can then be distributed amongst different coders as they work on several parts.

This is way beyond learning or writing code. It actually takes years of practice to acquire this skill. It's very much easier to code than to program. Of course, programmers know code, always knew code, but the same can't be said for coders, especially those who are just learning. Programming is used in a broader sense and coding is just one of the many processes of programming,

Coding is like writing a chapter, whereas programming is writing a book.

Programming involves deciding the right instructions and then providing instructions for a machine to carry it out, of course, with the expectation of a certain result, whereas coding is translating those predetermined instructions into a language the computer can understand.

Why You Should Learn How To Code

According to Strive Masiyiwa, the CEO of the Econet Group, basic coding, at least HTML, is something that everyone in this generation should learn. This is not a new saying, though; many people have spoken along these lines too. Coding has become a normal aspect of our lives. A lot of things we do have an aspect of coding or programming in them. So even if you don't intend becoming a career programmer, it's not a bad thing to have an idea of how some of the most common machines you use work. Most people don't have any idea of how the computer works. Here's the future of work, you'll either be told what to do by a computer or tell a computer what to do. And the only way to tell a computer what to do is by coding. We are getting to this place really fast, faster than you'd expect. Coding and programming in a way prepare you for these shifts and leaps in technologies. These leaps are not possible without coding. This is one very important reason you should learn how to code. You might never make a career out of it, but you'll be sure to understand what's going on in the world of technology around you.

CHAPTER 3:

Programming Languages and IDEs

I n this phase, we are going to discuss some of the many computer languages and programming IDEs that are available to use. At this point, this information is for setting up the long-term direction of children who are learning to code. These are tools that are used in real-world applications, but in many cases, there is no reason why children can't start learning to use these tools early. The same approach to programming can be used, starting off doing basic tasks and building up as time goes on, and children gain more experience. In the first phase, we will talk about the different computer languages that are used to give some familiarity with what's out there.

You can take this section with a little bit of a grain of salt. The reason I say that is computer languages are constantly evolving, and preferences and fads can come and go. That said, there are some core fundamental languages that should be learned at more advanced ages if the child is hoping to have some kind of career as a computer programmer or scientist.

The first is C++. This was probably the first object-oriented programming language, and it is still widely used. There are some aspects of the language that make it hard to learn for some people, but the advantage of learning it is that not only will you gain a valuable skill that is still used in a wide range of applications, but it also serves as a solid training ground that makes picking up other computer languages quite easy.

Java is also good to know. This is a language that is used in a lot of different applications, and its offshoot JavaScript is often used in web programming. Java was chosen as the language for apps made for the Android operating system, so knowing it is certainly going to be useful for job prospects since so many companies want to make Android apps.

Python is a great language to learn. The great thing about Python is that it's simple. It may be the simplest programming language that you can learn. After a child master's Scratch, learning Python is a definite next step. Furthermore, it's available on every computer system. If you have a Mac or a PC, you can get Python, and it might already be installed on your computers. You can learn all of the important concepts of computer programming using Python, including classes, lists, subroutines, functions, and more.

Ruby is a very popular programming language in the business world. It is one of the younger languages, C and C++ were developed long before Ruby came on the scene. Like Python, Ruby is considered easy to learn and use. Ruby can be used in a wide range of circumstances, including programming on the internet. This wide applicability is one thing that has generated a lot of its popularity. Ruby has been the backbone of many popular social media sites.

Finally, learning Swift, which is now the standard language for Apple apps for the iPhone, is a definite skill that children who are interested in becoming coders should learn. The beauty of Swift is that it's one of the easiest coding languages to learn.

The First Computer Languages

One of the first high-level languages that were developed is called Fortran. The purpose of this language was (and still is) to build programs for scientific purposes. Although it was first developed in the late 1950s, Fortran is still used today in many places. Fortran is really good at doing numerical calculations, and it is pretty easy to learn.

After Fortran was developed, some other languages were created to extend what high-level languages can do and to make coding easier. The first of these is a language called C. Like Fortran, C was developed largely for scientific and engineering purposes, but it is more sophisticated than Fortran. Since C can do a lot more, it quickly became more popular than Fortran.

Basic is another computer language that was developed at about the same time. The name is appropriate since the goal of creating Basic was to make a very easy to use computer language. Many who were using computers in business gravitated toward Basic since it was easy to learn and use. Basic is a very suitable programming language for children to learn on, but it is not nearly as popular as it once was.

As time went on, people who design computer languages and study computer science wanted to be able to better represent objects in the real world. This required them to change the way that computer languages were structured. This led them to create "object-oriented languages." The first of these that was developed is called C++. This became a pretty popular language, and it was based on the older c language, but it can model real-world objects like cars and airplanes (and even people) in computer code that languages like c can't. This language is still pretty popular, but other languages like Java were invented later, in some cases, to help people program the internet.

Python has become one of the most popular programming languages. It is a very simple language, building on the ideas behind the Basic language. However, it's a lot more sophisticated than Basic, and yet it maintains a lot of simplicity. Python is definitely suitable for use by children who are learning how to code. It is freely available for use on most computer systems.

Logic Errors

One of the most famous sayings in the computer programming world is garbage-in, garbage-out. It is possible to make errors in a computer program that are syntactically correct, and that also doesn't lead to bugs or crashes. But, they may generate the wrong answers. This can be a problem because these logic errors might be hard to track down or even recognize. Sometimes, the erroneous assumptions that the programmer has in their mind are programmed into the computer.

High-Level Tools for Video Games

Video games are one of the easiest ways to get children excited about coding. Since they enjoy playing video games, it's a natural fit for many to want to make them as well. There are many high-level tools for video games that let you draw out the video game on the screen. As you draw out each scene, you can add objects to the scene, exactly as you want them to appear in the game. Then you specify how each object should behave when the game is running.

Several tools are available that are quite similar to Scratch in the overall structure and function. They have scenes that can be drawn on the screen, and characters and objects can be position and moved around. Then the game designer can set up rules for each of the objects in the scene.

One of the first tools build in this way is called Game Salad. Game Salad is used as an educational tool to help teach children about computer science, and it can be used in a k-12 curriculum. But Game Salad is a real tool, and it can be used to create real games for devices like the iPhone. Game Salad lets you draw the game on the screen, and then set up rules for each object behind the scenes. Game Salad is actually quite similar to Scratch, and after a child has mastered Scratch, if they are in middle school or high school years using Game Salad will seem like a natural transition.

Another game building tool that some people use is called Corona. It uses a simple programming language call Lua. Corona is more coding based than the other tools we are describing in this phase; in fact, it is completely coding based. Many people prefer using this method, but these days being able to visualize your scenes and set them up without having to write code is a big step forward that saves a lot of work. That also helps the game developer focus on the actual design of the game itself, while with Lua, they are going to be getting lost in the coding details just to position objects on the screen and have them move about.

After Game Salad, more sophisticated game building tools were developed that are visually oriented. Buildbox is a very easy tool to use that is excellent for children. They can learn how to create games without coding at all, but they can also use "scripts" to specialize the code behind the scenes for their own games. Buildbox has been used to develop some of the most frequently downloaded apps on the Apple app store. A game is divided into a series of scenes, and you design each scene as if you were using PowerPoint or Keynote, specifying the properties of each object on the scene. It then compiles it into a working game for you. Buildbox comes in 2D and 3D versions. When using the 2D version, ordinary graphics can be imported into the development environment to set up backgrounds, characters, objects, and enemies. The design can actually get quite sophisticated using logic tools, and many different templates can help the designer build game mechanics that are similar to many successful chart-topping games.

The 3D version of the Buildbox is a little more sophisticated. Since it's a true 3D system, the objects in the games are actually meshes rather than image files. This version of Buildbox also lets designers get under the hood. Mind maps let you build up the behaviors of characters and other objects in the game, and you can actually work with the coding scripts of each element in the mind map. Those who master coding will be able to take advantage of these features in order to build up more sophisticated and complex games.

Unity 3D is the most sophisticated and popular tool used to build games for multiple platforms, including mobile, tablets, desktop computers, Apple TV, and Xbox. Unity is a middle ground tool, you build scenes visually on the screen, and set properties, but it also has coding behind it using a derivative of the C programming language called C# (C sharp). Unity developers are in high demand by the video gaming industry, so any children who are interested in careers as video game programmers can benefit by learning Unity, once they have learned to code very well in other contexts. Unity is powerful but a bit complicated. However, older children can begin learning Unity by following a careful course.

CHAPTER 4:

Debugging

D ebugging is the process or technique used to detect and eliminate problems that arise during writing and execution of a program. Since its incorporation in the 1940s, computer debugging has become one of the techniques used to prevent errors, bugs as well as mistakes arising during programming processes. The direct opposite of the term is anti-debugging, which entails reversing the method of detecting and removing such errors with tools like modified codes, API-based and timing, and latency.

In Python, the software also includes debugging but primarily depends on Python interpreter to reading, recognize, and eliminate problems. In some cases, Python debugging is quite effective and enables programmers to engage in the creation of programs after every breakpoint. When writing codes, you may continually input your codes without recognizing errors, bugs, or even typos that may affect your outcome. Therefore, debuggers tend to indicate these problems and may either provide solutions instantly or take a breaking point for you to correct it.

Process of Computer Debugging

Problems Identification and Reproduction

When writing codes, you begin writing from the command line, and you may either write continuously or the computer executing each command when a line is done. In this case, you may run into errors, and the debuggers are hence helpful. In this step, debuggers tend to recognize these mistakes and reproduce the problem to identify its viability. Either nontrivial or other bugs can be readily identified and later replicated to ascertain how they work and affect your coding processes.

Problem Generalization

Immediately your debugger has identified and determined that the problem is unnecessary in the program, it is then simplified by breaking the bug down for an effective elimination process. The benefit of breaking down this information is it ensures that your program does not crash when parsing or affecting other health values in the program. Breaking down of these files affected enhances the reproduction and subdivision of these bugs to ensure the problem is recognized easily. When these problems are generalized, you can now check them, including the source files, if they have errors and need immediate action to eliminate these problems.

Removal of the Problem

The next step is to eliminate the problem using a debugger tool after a successful reproduction and simplification of the errors. The tool will scan your values, including the provision of a complete analysis of your files suspected to cause the problem. Removing the issue at the point of origin is essential as it enables you to quickly realize the source files and manage or eliminate them to avoid future occurrences of these problems. In Python, recognizing and removing coding questions usually promotes the execution of high-performance programs.

Python Debugging Tools

There are several tools used today in Python for debugging and may be confused with others; therefore essential to learn about them. The tools may, however, differ in functioning depending on the operating system you have or the level of errors available in the program. Some people may tend to have more than one debugging tool with the objective of completely doing away with problems when creating their desirable programs.

Debuggers

Debugger tools, especially for Python, exist in two forms, specific tools, and multipurpose tools, depending on the program length and operating system. Some of the all-purpose debugger tools include PdbRcldea and pdb, and versatile tools include trepan2, epdb, and Winpdb, which primarily focus on the errors originating from different areas. On the other hand, specific debugger tools include DDD, Xpdb, and gdb, which identify and eliminate mistakes from particular regions. These debugger tools work in different areas, which may include during variable naming, program creation, execution, or when writing codes.

Integrated Development Environment (IDEs)

This is one of the most used debugging tools, preferably used in advanced and large projects by experienced developers. The IDEs Python debugging tools may vary of the functionality, but features accompanied usually remain the same. They also identify and eliminate programming errors in different sections, including when running your codes, evaluating variables, and designing breakpoints. The PyCharm is the commonly used debugging tool type of IDEs consisting of all the components such as plugs to maximize problem identification, simplification, and elimination.

Special-Purpose

This is another type of Python debugging tool suitable for detecting and eliminating bugs situated in the remote sections of the program. They are essential in tracing flaws and mistakes created in sensitive areas where other debugging tools are unable to detect. Some of them include FirePython used by Firefox in performing deep scans to remove hidden errors. This is one of the vital Python debugging tools which ensure that programmers do not get stuck because of mistakes originating from unknown locations within the program. As such, special-purpose debugging tools provide a conducive working environment for programmers to create applications without facing challenges arising from inconspicuous areas.

Below are some benefits of learning to code with Python:

- **Easier and better debugging:**

Debugging refers to a process of searching for bugs and defects and resolving them. These bugs and errors tend to inhibit a program or system from working correctly. In this vein, debugging aims to resolve problems in programs. In terms of debugging, Python is one of the highest-ranking programming languages owing to the tools it provides, such as PyDebug, pudb, and pdb, which help make the debugging experience smooth and manageable.

Take, for instance, the tool—pudb can help programmers analyze the core of codes and track down a problem. When compared, while other languages keep working to improve their debugging experiences and tools, Python only gets better with time.

- **There are no restrictions to its programming syntax:**

Unlike other programming languages, Python can be easily understood by anyone, even up to a non-programmer. The reason is primarily attributed to its high readability and problem-oriented design, which lets one pay attention to coding logically rather than expressly delving into the nitty-gritty of the syntax.

As proof of this unique benefit, consider the sample program shown below to calculate a simple interest. Taking a look at the program, you can note how relatively easy it is to decode and write the code in Python.

- **An explicit declaration is not required:**

When coding in Python, type specifiers should not be used in the declaration of variables because it can be done without declaring any of the data types in Python. Additionally, it is unnecessary to make use of separators, such as semicolons (;) in marking the end of a statement or command. Indentation in Python takes the place of parenthesis in grouping a block of code. And to make indentations in codes, you can make use of either spaces or tabs. Albeit, some rules are enforced in Python, like the use of four spaces for each level of indentation. Many other facets of Python, such as this, contribute to making learning easier for beginners.

- **Great Object-oriented programming support:**

Object-oriented programming comes as a built-in element in Python. It creates a model to produce solutions by devising objects, binding data, and defining connections. Albeit, the procedural programming makes it different approach from top to bottom, solving one challenge at once and splitting it into bit sizes. Object-oriented programming, on the one hand, is a different ball game altogether. It adopts a bottom to top problem-solving approach that looks for blueprints to the solution from the onset, thereby leaving implementation to a much later time.

To develop yourself as an expert Python programmer, constructing objects, building inheritance, and using classes are fundamental approaches to take. What's more, is that these concepts can be easily mastered in Python for the production of quality programs with quicker implementations than other programming languages. Python encourages minimalism in code sizes, allowing for faster and better applications.

CHAPTER 5:

Loops

Loops are going to be another great topic that we are able to work with when it comes to Python. Loops are a good way to clean up some of the code that you want to work with so that you can make sure that enough shows up in your code, without having to write out as many lines. For example, if you have a code that you would like to work with, that lists out the numbers going one from fifty, you do not want to actually write out that many lines of code in the process. You can work with these loops instead, to make sure that it is able to write out the lines, but it is really just a short amount of code. These loops are then able to hold onto a ton of information and will only use a few lines of code to make it happen.

There are a lot of things and a ton of data that we are then able to add into the loop, but you will find that these are actually pretty easy for us to work with anyway. These loops are going to be there to tell the compiler that it needs to continue reading through one or two lines of code over and over again until the conditions that you add into it are met.

So, if you are working on a program where you ask the compiler to write out numbers that go from one to ten, then the loop will tell your compiler to read through the numbers going from one to ten, then the loop will be set to go through the same line of code until it reaches ten. This can simplify the code while making sure that you are still able to get the things done that you would like.

When you work with all of these loops, it is important to remember to set up so that you have the condition in place before you ever try to work on the program. If you just go through and write out your loop, without adding in the condition that is needed, then the loop will start, but it will not know when to stop. The loop will just keep going through itself and will freeze the computer. Double-check before you run the program that the condition is in place before starting.

As you go through and create some of your own code with Python, there is going to be a few different loop types that you are able to work with. There are actually going to be many options, but we need to focus on the three main ones known as the while loop, the for loop, and the nested loop.

The While Loop

The first type of loop that we are going to work on is the while loop. This loop is one that you can choose for your code when you know the specific number of times you want the code to cycle through that loop. You would use it to finish counting to ten, for example. This one will need to have a condition, in the end, to make sure that it stops at the right point and doesn't keep going forever. It is also a good option if you want to ensure that your loop occurs at least one time before it moves on to the next part of the code. A good example of the while loop is the following code:

#calculation of simple interest. Ask the user to input the principal, rate of interest, number of years.

Counter = 1

While (counter <= 3):

Principal = into (input ("Enter the principal amount :"))

Numberofyeras = int (input ("Enter the number of years :"))

Rateofinterest = float (input ("Enter the rate of interest : "))

Simple interest = principal * numberofyears * rateofinterest/100

Print ("Simple interest = %.2f" %simpleinterest)

#increase the counter by 1

counter = counter + 1

Print ("You have calculated simple interest for 3 time!")

With the example that we did above, you will find that the user is able to place in the information that makes the most sense for them and the program. The code is then going to give them the interest rate based on the information that the user provides to it. For this one, we are going to set up the while at the beginning of the code and then told it to only go through the loop a maximum of three times. You will then be able to change up the code as well to make sure that it will go through the loops as many times as you would like.

Working On the For Loop

The While Loop can help us out with a lot of the different things that you want to accomplish when you are working on loops in this part of the code. In addition to handling some of the work with loops that the While Loop can do, it is possible to work with them for a loop. When you are working with the For Loops, you are working with the method that is considered the more traditional out of the two, and you can even make this the option that you use all of the time.

When you work with one of the For Loops, your user will not go in and provide information to the code, and then the loops start. Rather, with the For Loop, Python is set up to go through an iteration in the order that it shows up on the screen. There is no need for input from the user because it just continues through the iteration until the end occurs. An example of a code that shows how a For Loop works is the following:

Measure strings word to:

Words = ['apple', 'mango', 'Bannana', 'orange']

For w in words:

Print (w, Len (w))

Write this code into your compiler and then execute it. The For Loop is going to make sure that all the words in the line above it, are shown up on the screen, exactly how you wrote them out. If you want them in a different order, you need to do that as you work on the code, not later on. You can add in any words or other information that you want to show up in this kind of loop, just make sure that you have it in the right order from the beginning.

The Nested Loop

We can also finish this out with a look at how the nested loop is going to work. This is a more advanced type of loop that is going to combine two of the other loop types together in order to get them to run at the same time. There are a number of instances where you can work with this nested loop, and it is often going to depend on the kind of code that you would like to complete and what you are hoping to get out of it.

The third type of loop that we are able to work with here is going to be known as the Nested Loop. Any time that you are working with this loop, you are basically going to take one of the other types of loops, and then you will place it inside of a different loop. Both of these loops will end up running in the code at the same time, and they will both continue on until they are complete. There are a number of situations where you will want to focus on these Nested Loops to help you finish your code.

For example, you may find that you would like to work on a nested loop that can create a new multiplication table, the Nested Loop is going to be a good one to get it done. The code that we need to use in order to make this one work for our needs and to see how a Nested Loop is going to work will include:

#write a multiplication table from 1 to 10

For x in xrange (1, 11):

For y in xrange (1, 11):

Print '%d = %d' % (x, y, x*x)

When you got the output of this program, it is going to look similar to this:

1*1 = 1

1*2 = 2

1*3 = 3

1*4 = 4

All the way up to 1*10 = 2

Then it would move on to do the table by twos such as this:

2*1 =2

2*2 = 4

And so on until you end up with 10*10 = 100 as your final spot in the sequence

Any time you need to get one loop to run inside another loop, the Nested Loop will be able to help you get this done. You can combine together the For Loop, the While Loop, or each combination based on what you want to get done inside the code. But it definitely shows you how much time and space inside the code that these loops can save. The multiplication table above only took up four lines to write out and you got a huge table. Think of how long this would take if you had to write out each part of the table!

The For Loop, the While Loop, and the Nested Loop are going to be some of the most common loops that a beginner is able to focus on when it is time to write out their own codes in this language. You are able to use these codes to make sure that you can get a ton done in some of the programs that you have chosen, without having to focus as much on writing out a ton of lines. You are even able to do this in a manner that will make sure that certain parts of the code will read through themselves again, without you having to rewrite it at all. There are many times when you will want to handle writing loops in your code, and learning how to make each one work can help make your code stronger.

CHAPTER 6:

What Programming Language Should You Learn?

So we've seen what could be said to be the basics. What coding is and what it is not, programming language, markup and styling languages, and perhaps many other things in-between. So now, I believe you're ready to learn code. And you've learned enough terminologies so that the words we use here will not fly past your head. And even if they do, it's okay; this is a book and not a test; therefore, you could always go back and relearn. That's actually one of the things you'll learn as a coder. You'll actually never arrive at the place where you can say that you know it all. As far as coding is concerned, there's always something new, some update, or the other. It could be a new programming language or just a new way to do old things, faster, better, and perhaps cooler.

So, where does one start? There are so many programming languages. Which is the best? What programming language should you learn? These are some of the questions people ask the most when it comes to coding. I remember telling my friend to teach me how to code. And he asked me a question along these lines.

Fact is told, there are no best programming languages; at least we don't look at them that way. Programming languages are tools to enable us to achieve certain objectives. And depending on the task at hand, we'll pick the tool that we think we are most deft with or that is most efficient for the task at hand. Now that's the way you should look at coding.

So to answer the question, what tool should you learn first? Well, it all depends on the task that you'll want to carry out.

Why Do You Want To Learn Coding?

What do you intend to be able to do with your coding skills? Do you fancy being able to hack into NASA's firewall? (Now this is supposed to be a joke, don't try it, even if you have the skills, there'll most likely be hell to pay.) Ok, now, seriously, what do you envisage yourself doing with your coding skills? Do you desire to build websites, or do you want to build games and create mobile apps. Do you desire to work in Crypto or be an AI engineer? Are you interested in building Robots or maybe sending satellites to space? Could it be you are interested in cybersecurity, or you actually want to be a hacker? Not all hackers are bad guys; by the way, there are some who are called ethical hackers. And these guys are actually very, very useful. They ensure web portals and other online stuff are safe. Now, if you don't know what you'd like to do with your programming knowledge, that's fine too.

However, knowing what you'd like to do or those things that you'd like to do (who said that it has to be one thing) will make it easier for you to make a decision as to the language to learn or what to specialize in. If you probably had no idea about what you wanted from coding, I have just mentioned a few above, and that can give you an idea of what can be done with coding.

You must also be aware of what you're ready to commit to learning code. How much time, how much money, and how much energy are you willing to commit to learning code. If you want an intensive class with support, then you'll have to be willing to pay for it. However, you can also get free classes; there are actually loads of websites and online spaces that offer these. We'll look at some of them in a subsequent Phase. Next, we'll be talking about the various categories of things that can be done with coding and the languages you need to learn to do those things.

Web Development

This has got to be the most popular of all the cool stuff code can be made to do. The fact that it is popular doesn't make it any less important. In fact, did you know that there are over 1.5 billion websites in the world today, this is according to internetlivestats.com. People wrote codes for those sites, and people have to maintain them and upgrade them. In fact, web development is the widest sort after skills for people looking for the service of developers. Website development can be divided into 3; Front-end development, back-end development, and full-stack development.

1. **Front-end Developers:** These are those who are involved with coding that part of the websites we can see. So everything you see on a website when you open it, the images, fonts, the layout, everything is done by Front-end developers. The minimum languages need for Front-end development, or web designing is HTML, CSS, and JavaScript. With mastery of these tools, you can build a professional-looking website. Of course, being able to use jQuery, Git, and Github, other libraries and frameworks will be an added advantage for you.

Front-end development also includes UI/UX design, which is a user interface/user experience design. This is like the web page/app layout. What it looks like, the color scheme, font size, and style, how interactive and responsive the website is. In some cases, what the person feels when they get on the site. Front-end development is not just about writing code; a lot of designing also goes into it. Front-end developers would a lot of times have to meet with non-technical persons, and so as to get their ideas and feel about the website they are working on. If you want to learn Front-end development, you also have to build your communication skills, and maybe understand a bit of human psychology. Some of the best UI/UX designers understand or have studied psychology. This will help you read and understand people, or know how people think, which will help you build interfaces and experiences that they'd love. It's not going to be out of place to learn graphic design software such as Adobe Photoshop, Sketch or other design software.

So if you're more interested in aesthetics, style, you like colors, and color schemes, interface design, and layout, then this might just be something you might want to try.

2. **Back-end Development:** This is like the foundation of a website. That is the behind the scenes structures (such as databases, web servers, and applications) of the web site that makes it work. This kind of development involves the writing of the core website logic. It involves getting the appropriate data from the database, deciding how it is used and displayed to the user, using the Front-end. There are quite a number of languages used for Back-end development. They include PHP, Python, Ruby on Rails, Node.js, and many more. A back-end developer must be able to understand how to extract data from database engines like MySQL, PostgreSQL, and many more. If you are very logical in nature, you like to solve puzzles, you pay attention to detail and are methodological in your approach to doing things, and this might just be a career path for you.

3. **Full-stack Development:** Here's an enviable position and skill too. A full-stack developer basically can do both Front-end and Back-end development. Such fellows are mighty useful in website projects because they can contribute ideas and code all the step of the way. So these fellows know HTML, CSS, and JavaScript, and also Back-end programming languages.

151

How Websites Work

We've seen the different fields involved in web development; it's only apt, I think, that you get a rough idea of how a website works. First things first, what is web development. For a developer or someone in tech, this is supposed to be a no brainer. But not all of us work in tech. So in the next few lines, we'll be exploring this topic, of course, first with some little background.

Just the same way every individual person is unique, but share the basic functions of the human body such as reproductive systems, respiratory systems, this is also a way one can describe websites. Each website could be said to be unique in its own individual way. However, there are basic components every website has. These are:

Client: This is the device in which you are using to access the internet at a particular time. So this could be your desktop, laptop, phone, or tablet.

Server: This is some sort of hard disk, or computer, a remote one though that contains all the files and codes that make a website run.

Database: This is also part of the remote server; it stores dynamic information used or generated on a website. So account information of website users, log in details, and all of that. Here's a way to explain the working of websites and the internet.

So let's assume Mike wants to visit Quora.com.

- Mike types Quora website into the browser of his phone (the client).

- His phone generates and sends a request to the remote server.

- The server acts on the request, takes data from the database, and then sends it back to the server. All these happen at the Back-end.

- Next, the server uses the data and produces a response with the use of front-end code.

- Finally, the response is sent to the client (Mike's phone), where it is then seen as Quora's home page.

CHAPTER 7:

Pre-Schoolers Offline Coding

Nowadays, it feels like babies are born with the ability to work a computer. Indeed, my youngest child was able to download apps and play them by himself by the age of about two and a half, simply by watching his older brother and copying what he did on his tablet.

However, I wouldn't recommend sitting a child as young as two or three down in front of a computer to teach them a computer programming language and expect them to pick it up. Indeed, even with older children, it is far better to learn the basics in a way that is hands-on. In fact, you don't even need a computer to teach children the basics of coding. I know, it sounds crazy, right? Offline coding allows children to explore the concepts in a way that is fun and allows them to process it in their own way, relating them to real-life experiences.

Another benefit of offline coding is that you can add these experiences into their everyday lives or in a school setting. They can be an added dimension to, say, a mathematics or English lesson.

Offline coding can get a child interested in computer programming that may not otherwise want to sit in front of a computer and look at jargon for hours on end.

Plus, there's no guilt about how much time children spend in front of a computer, which means you can add in coding experiences more regularly during the day or week, and children don't even have to know that they are learning coding unless you wish to tell them.

Pre-Schoolers

I will add in a note about pre-schoolers here because even though parents often say they aren't going to let their toddlers use computers or tablets, there is no denying that some of these products are becoming geared toward this age group. I'm not going to go into the pros and cons of it or start a debate about whether a two-year-old should be bought a tablet or not, but I do believe there are benefits if they are used in moderation.

While I didn't grow up with a computer in my hand, I feel that my children's generation is being brought up that way and that it does benefit them to know how to use computers; the future is becoming more and more technology-based and, therefore, their generation is going to be engrossed in it.

Computers weren't really used when I was a child, so as a teenager we were taught the very basics, such as how to turn the computer on, open Word Documents or set up a spreadsheet, and so on. While this may still be taught in ICT lessons, I think the presumption is that most children understand how to turn on a computer and open a program. Tablets are becoming more common in classroom settings, and I can only presume that eventually it will be assumed that children can do the basics and what is taught in schools will start a bit further along, therefore teaching them at a young age at home means they won't be at a disadvantage.

Again, this doesn't mean I would recommend sitting down a toddler and teaching them Scratch or using computer jargon with them. You aren't physically going to teach your toddler and pre-schooler coding, but you can teach them logical thinking and problem solving, which are skills needed for coding, and this can be done with inset puzzles and floor puzzles. These are, in essence, problem-solving tasks that allow children to examine smaller pieces to make a bigger picture; a foundation of coding is the ability to break a big problem down into small steps.

TangRams

TangRams are also great for exploring shapes and solving problems; can children make a certain shape or picture? You can start by getting younger children to match up the shapes to a board and talk with them about what the picture is. Then move on to have them copy a pattern or picture that you make. Then have them making up their own pictures and patterns.

Building Blocks

Building blocks are also a great toy for budding engineers and computer programmers. After all, building something out of blocks takes a lot of determination and patience, especially for a toddler who is just starting to refine their motor skills. It also requires logical thinking to figure out how blocks can be placed, which pieces fit on top of each other, and which ones don't. If it topples, they have to rebuild it, but work out a way that they can do so without it falling down again. Learning patience will be an extremely helpful skill for coding.

Dominos

Domino chains help children to understand cause and effect. Stand the dominos on their sides to make a line or a pattern on the floor; what happens if one falls?

At this age and stage of a child's development, you don't even need to relate it to coding and computers, you are just trying to install patience and logical thinking for the future.

Games like Simon Says, Mother May I? As well as board games can help children think logically and follow instructions.

Reading stories can help pre-schoolers understand sequencing.

These types of toys can be used for teaching older children just by extending them, which will be explained in more detail later.

Copying Games

Back to Back Copying

These games are great for learning to give step by step directions and learning how to break these down into small steps, as well as showing the importance of giving these steps in a methodical way.

One person gives an instruction and the other one copies. The goal is to replicate something that the person giving the instructions is looking at. This can be a model that they have made out of Lego, wooden blocks, a 2D shape picture, or a simple drawing.

This game is best played in pairs. The players sit back to back or have a board between them so they can't see what the other person is doing. The child can make the model or picture first, or you can give it to them. Again, this depends on context, age, and ability.

Let's say you are playing at home with your child using wooden blocks. You have made a structure. Now you have to describe this to the child for them to replicate, so you might say first place a blue cuboid/rectangle on its end, next place a cube/square on top. You can specify color or just use shape.

While it sounds like an easy game, if the person giving the instructions isn't exact, the person following can end up with an entirely different structure.

Learning Objectives

This teaches the importance of giving instructions precisely and in the correct order and demonstrates what happens if something isn't sequenced correctly.

It is a fun game that also consolidates mathematical concepts such as positional language and shape names.

Color on Command

For this game, you need a stack of cards with different directions written on them. These can be as simple as arrows.

Give the child some graph paper with large squares or just draw squares on yourself. The bigger the squares, the quicker the game will be; the smaller the squares, the longer it will last, so this will again be dependent on age. You can draw the squares by hand or do it on the computer.

Let the child choose where to start. This can be a square in the middle of the piece of paper or at an edge or corner. When they have collared it in, they pick a card and follow the direction, so if it is an arrow that says forward one, then they color the next square along. If it says turn right or left, they choose a square to the right or left of the one they have just collared.

You can add in 'debugging' concepts if they pick a card that then takes them off the edge of the page. Simply say something like, "Uh-oh, there's a bug, we need to re-program the pen by choosing a different card."

If you want to make this more challenging, then you can add in "If"/Then statements such as "If you choose a card that is forwards THEN you color the square in red." "If you choose a card that says turn THEN you color the square in blue."

Math Codes

You can add in a bit of mathematics practice while playing these coding games, as well. This can be either as part of a treasure hunt or just written down on paper for the fun of solving them. You can add in an extra challenge by saying, "How many can you solve in three/five/ten minutes?" and setting a timer.

For example, using the numbers instead of a letters code, where A = 1 and B = 2, you can leave spaces or draw a line for each letter and underneath write a maths sum. The child works out the sum, which gives them a number, which they then have to translate into a letter.

An example of I LOVE YOU would be:

— —————— —— ——— ———

3x3 15-3 5x311x2 10-530-5 30-15 20 − 1

So 3x3 = 9, this corresponds to the letter I. 15 − 3 = 12, which corresponds to the letter L and so on. Of course, these are just examples. Make the sums as easy or difficult as you want, depending on the age and ability of the children. For five and six year Old's, you may want to use minus and addition sums; for older children who are familiar with multiplication and division, you can start using those.

Learning Outcomes

By working out written codes, children are problem-solving and refining their logical thinking skills. There is an element of literacy and mathematics if using number, letter, or symbol codes. They are also working in a methodical way. For example, to decipher your code with a code wheel, they need to try different options until the correct one is apparent.

At home, working with a sibling or an adult or in a classroom situation, children who are working together to solve these puzzles and codes are also using their collaboration and teamwork skills.

Encouraging children to design their own codes helps them be creative.

CHAPTER 8:

Working with Files

Programs are made with input and output in mind.

You input data to the program, the program processes the input, and it ultimately provides you with output.

For example, a calculator will take in numbers and operations you want.

It will then process the operation you wanted.

And then, it will display the result to you as its output.

There are multiple ways for a program to receive input and to produce output.

One of those ways is to read and write data on files.

To start learning how to work with files, you need to learn the open () function.

The open () function has one required parameter and two optional parameters.

The first and required parameter is the file name.

The second parameter is the access mode.

And the third parameter is buffering or buffer size.

The filename parameter requires string data.

The access mode requires string data, but there is a set of string values that you can use and is defaulted to "r."

The buffer size parameter requires an integer and is defaulted to 0.

To practice using the open () function, create a file with the name sampleFile.txt inside your Program directory.

Try this sample code:

```
>>> file1 = open ("sampleFile.txt")

>>> _
```

Note that the file function returns a file object.

The statement in the example assigns the file object to variable file1.

The file object has multiple attributes, and three of them are:

- Name: This contains the name of the file.

- Mode: This contains the access mode you used to access the file.

- Closed: This returns False if the file has been opened and True if the file is closed. When you use the open() function, the file is set to open.

Now, access those attributes.

>>> file1 = open("sampleFile.txt")

>>> file1.name

'sampleFile.txt'

>>> file1.mode

'r'

>>> file1.closed

False

>>> _

Whenever you are finished with a file, close them using the close() method.

>>> file1 = open("sampleFile.txt")

```
>>> file1.closed
```

False

```
>>> file1.close()
```

```
>>> file1.closed
```

True

```
>>> _
```

Remember that closing the file does not delete the variable or object.

To reopen the file, just open and reassign the file object.

For example:

```
>>> file1 = open("sampleFile.txt")
```

```
>>> file1.close()
```

```
>>> file1 = open(file1.name)
```

```
>>> file1.closed
```

False

```
>>> _
```

Reading from a File

Before proceeding, open the sampleFile.txt in your text editor.

Type "Hello World" in it and save.

Go back to Program.

To read the contents of the file, use the read() method.

For example:

>>> file1 = open("sampleFile.txt")

>>> file1.read()

'Hello World'

>>> _

File Pointer

Whenever you access a file, Program sets the file pointer.

The file pointer is like your word processor's cursor.

Any operation on the file starts at where the file pointer is.

When you open a file, and when it is set to the default access mode, which is "r" (read-only), the file pointer is set at the beginning of the file.

To know the current position of the file pointer, you can use the tell()
method.

For example:

>>> file1 = open("sampleFile.txt")

>>> file1.tell()

0

>>> _

Most of the actions you perform on the file move the file pointer.

For example:

>>> file1 = open("sampleFile.txt")

>>> file1.tell()

0

>>> file1.read()

'Hello World'

>>> file1.tell()

11

```
>>> file1.read()
```

"

```
>>> _
```

To move the file pointer to a position you desire, you can use the seek()
function.

For example:

```
>>> file1 = open("sampleFile.txt")
```

```
>>> file1.tell()
```

0

```
>>> file1.read()
```

'Hello World'

```
>>> file1.tell()
```

11

```
>>> file1.seek(0)
```

0

```
>>> file1.read()
```

'Hello World'

>>> file1.seek(1)

1

>>> file1.read()

'ello World'

>>> _

The seek() method has two paRameters.

The first is offset, which sets the pointer's position depending on the second paRameter.

Also, argument for this parameter is required.

The second parameter is optional.

It is for whence, which dictates where the "seek" will start.

It is set to 0 by default.

- If set to 0, Program will set the pointer's position to the offset argument.

- If set to 1, Program will set the pointer's position relative or in addition to the current position of the pointer.

- If set to 2, Program will set the pointer's position relative or in addition to the file's end.

Note that the last two options require the access mode to have binary access.

If the access mode does not have binary access, the last two options will be useful to determine the current position of the pointer [seek(0, 1)] and the position at the end of the file [seek(0, 2)].

For example:

>>> file1 = open("sampleFile.txt")

>>> file1.tell()

0

>>> file1.seek(1)

1

>>> file1.seek(0, 1)

0

>>> file1.seek(0, 2)

11

>>> _

File Access Modes

To write to a file, you will need to know more about file access modes in Program.

There are three types of file operations: reading, writing, and appending.

Reading allows you to access and copy any part of the file's content.

Writing allows you to overwrite a file's contents and create a new one.

Appending allows you to write on the file while keeping the other content intact.

There are two types of file access modes: string and binary.

String access allows you to access a file's content as if you are opening a text file.

Binary access allows you to access a file on its rawest form: binary.

In your sample file, accessing it using string access allows you to read the line "Hello World."

Accessing the file using binary access will let you read "Hello World" in binary, which will be b'Hello World'.

For example:

```
>>> x = open("sampleFile.txt", "rb")

>>> x.read()

b'Hello World'

>>> _
```

String access is useful for editing text files.

Binary access is useful for anything else, like pictures, compressed files, and executables. In this book, you will only be taught how to handle text files.

There are multiple values that you can enter in the file access mode parameter of the open() function.

But you do not need to memorize the combination.

You just need to know the letter combinations.

Each letter and symbol stands for an access mode and operation.

For example:

- r = read-only—file pointer placed at the beginning

  o   r+ = read and write

- a = append—file pointer placed at the end

- o   a+ = read and append

- • w = overwrite/create—file pointer set to 0 since you create the file

- o   w+ = read and overwrite/create

- • b = binary

By default, file access mode is set to string.

You need to add b to allow binary access.

For example: "rb."

Writing to a File

When writing to a file, you must always remember that Program overwrites and not insert file.

For example:

>>> x = open("sampleFile.txt", "r+")

>>> x.read()

'Hello World'

>>> x.tell(0)

0

```
>>> x.write("text")

4

>>> x.tell()

4

>>> x.read()

'o World'

>>> x.seek(0)

0

>>> x.read()

'texto World'

>>> _
```

You might have expected that the resulting text will be "textHello World".

The write method of the file object replaces each character one by one, starting from the current position of the pointer.

Practice Exercise

For practice, you need to perform the following tasks:

- Create a new file named test.txt.

- Write the entire practice exercise instructions on the file.

- Close the file and reopen it.

- Read the file and set the cursor back to 0.

- Close the file and open it using append access mode.

- Add a rewritten version of these instructions at the end of the file.

- Create a new file and put similar content to it by copying the contents of the test.txt file.

Summary

Working with files in Program is easy to understand but difficult to implement.

As you already saw, there are only a few things that you need to remember.

The hard part is when you are actually accessing the file.

Remember that the key things that you should master are the access modes and the management of the file pointer.

It is easy to get lost in a file that contains a thousand characters.

Aside from being versed with the file operations, you should also supplement your learning with the functions and methods of the str class in Program.

Most of the time, you will be dealing with strings if you need to work on a file.

Do not worry about binary yet.

That is a different beast altogether and you will only need to tame it when you are already adept at Program.

As a beginner, expect that you will not deal yet with binary files that often contain media information.

Anyway, the next lesson is an elaboration on the "try" and "except" statements.

You'll discover how to manage and handle errors and exceptions effectively.

CHAPTER 9:

Conditionals

Many times, at the time of programming, it is considered necessary to make the decision about whether or not we should execute a specific piece of the program, and even in a given condition, it is necessary to execute several pieces of code. It is the text terminal and the standard input is the keyboard.

For this type of case, we have the sentences called "if," "else," and "elif."

Conditionals such as if, else, and elif, in Python are mostly used to execute an instruction in the case of certain conditions, in which one or more are met. We can see the conditional as the moment in which the decisions to take in our program are presented; depending on them, the program can be executed or not.

It is very important to understand correctly the use of conditionals since they will be the basis for our programs to be dynamic and perform certain tasks according to their condition. Since as you know, the programs are not as simple as you imagine, they will gradually become more complicated codes, but do not worry, practice will achieve success.

The "If" Statement

This statement is responsible for evaluating a logical operation, which can give a result of the type "True" or "False" and then executes a certain piece of code as long as its result is true.

Now, how can we see this? Well, this statement is very useful when programming. Between these statements and loops, we can cover a large part of the codes that exist today, so it is of the highest importance to understand the "if." Imagine the hypothetical case that you are presenting an admission exam to a university, and there is a program designed to enter the grades of all those who have presented the exam and to indicate whether it is admitted or not. If the grade is greater or equal to the expected value to enter the university, the same program will be responsible for placing the student in the database as a new entry to the university, but in the opposite case, nothing will be done and move to the next.

The syntax of the "if" is as follows:

```
1   x = 14
2   y = 21
3   if y > x:
4      print("y is bigget than x")
```

We observe that a simple evaluation of two variables "x" and "y" is made, the condition of the program will be that, if the condition is fulfilled, the program prints us the text; otherwise it does nothing.

This conditional could be interpreted as:

- If the young person is of legal age, he or she can enter the club.

- If the student passed his exams, he has passed the subject.

- If the consumer has already paid, he can withdraw his order.

Another case we can use, which is very important, is to apply this knowledge to real life, the same cases, could be the calculation of the area of a rectangle or can also be the calculation of a division. The same ones can be used, but there are cases in which the same ones can fall in errors and can be processed with an "if"; let's see the following examples to know a bit more of what we are talking about.

```
if.py      ×

1    h=input("The height of the rectangle: ")
2    b=input("The base of the rectangle: ")
3    h=int(h)
4    b=int(b)
5    if(h>=0 and b>=0):
6        a=b*h
7        a=str(a)
8        print("The result is: "+a)
9    print("Bye")
```

The first thing we can observe in this example is that two variables were initialized, both h and b, which are input type, one is related to the height of the rectangle, and the other is related to the width of the base, respectively.

Immediately afterwards, what we did was to convert these variables into integers, since, at the moment of initializing them, they are a string, because this is how inputs are defined, it is important to note that when the input function is used, the variable that is associated to it becomes a string type; when observing this, it is necessary to make the variables integers, since it is not possible to perform mathematical operations with ASCII characters but with numbers, whether decimal, binary or hexadecimal; for that reason, the int() function is used, which converts the string that is as an argument, into an integer.

Already, at the moment of arriving at the condition of the if, we take into account two events that are related and to occur simultaneously, in order to be able to proceed to make the mathematical calculations; they are: first that h is greater than zero, and also, that b is greater than zero, Why that? Well, everything has to happen simultaneously, because if not, three things can happen:

- $h<0$, which indicates that a negative area may arise.

- $b<0$, which indicates that we will also have a negative area.

- $b<0$ and $h<0$, and even if we find an area greater than zero, it is not good to say that a measure of length is less than zero.

When observing this, the only valid condition is the one mentioned recently, which is that the two length measurements are greater than zero simultaneously. And at the moment that this condition is True, we proceed to enter into the if block, within which, we proceed to calculate the area of the rectangle, then convert the variable into a string, and finally print on the screen the value of the area of the rectangle.

Finally, "Bye" was printed on the screen in order to know that the program has been successfully completed.

Now, we can also make another example, which is very useful at the moment of dividing, since it is known that the division between zero is not defined; therefore, we have to force that the denominator is different from zero, as we can see next.

```
d=int(input("Please enter a number for the denominator: "))
n=int(input("Please enter a number for the numerator: "))
if(d!=0):
    print("Result:"+str(n/d))
print("OK")
```

The first thing we can see in this example is that we declare two variables: the first is the one we call d, the same is related to the denominator of the division, on the other hand, the variable n, is from the numerator of the division; it is clearly seen that a precondition of the program is that a number must be entered, any, logically, the denominator different from zero, but does not have any other restriction. A curious thing that we can find in the code is that it uses the function int(), and then, within it, the function input, and...Why? Well, because as you should know, the variable input, returns a string, which depends on the input the user wants, therefore, what we proceed to do is convert the string into an integer in a more compact way in code.

Then, the condition that must be met is that the denominator should be different from zero, or specifically in code, that the variable d, should be different from zero. In the case that this condition is fulfilled, the obtained result will be printed on the screen, but you may observe that the string "Result:" is concatenated with the string resulting from the division between n and d.

Finally, it is printed on the screen to show that the program has finished in the correct way, and there is nothing to worry about.

Else Statement

This statement could be seen as a plug-in to the "if" statement since it provides you with other code alternatives when executing a program if its evaluated expression is of the "False" type.

Then we can say that this sentence is very necessary, since it is the case in which a condition is not met and you want to perform an action because of that, because as we saw in the example above, specifically in the areas or the division, something more is needed, that can be intuited because it is true, no error was made, but it needs something to tell the user that he entered some wrong value. This is one of the reasons why an "else" is necessary, but not only that, we can also take this to another level; imagine that you are programming the communication of a fuel plant and in the hypothesis that the condition is that if there is no spill, a green led will turn on, but in the case that this is not true, and the else does not exist, then it would be a real disaster; therefore, in that case, we introduce an "else" to notify customers that a problem is occurring in the plant.

The syntax for "else" is as follows:

```
1   x = 21
2   y = 14
3   if y > x:
4       print("y is bigger than x")
5   else:
6       print("x is bigger than y")
7
```

In this case, we can observe that it is similar to the "if" case, but there is a case in which the condition of the "if" is going to be of the "False" type. If this case had been presented to us in the example, our program would have remained in the air without any response, in this one we will have the "else" that will give another way to the program in which it will be of the "True" type, and this one will be able to continue executing.

This conditional could be interpreted as an escape to a sentence if and we can see it as:

- If the young man is of legal age, he can enter the club. If not, it will have to move away from the entrance.

- If the student passed his exams, he has passed the subject. If not, the subject must be retaken.

- If the consumer has already paid, he can withdraw his order. If not, he must pay before consuming.

We cannot leave aside the other examples of the if because, in this case, they are also important. We will focus first, in the example of the area of the rectangle:

```
if.py                    ✕

1    h=input("The height of the rectangle: ")
2    b=input("The base of the rectangle: ")
3    h=int(h)
4    b=int(b)
5    if(h>=0 and b>=0):
6        a=b*h
7        a=str(a)
8        print("The result is: "+a)
9    else:
10       print("Error")
11   print("Bye")
12
```

In this example, we can observe that, in an analogous way as it is done in the example of the if that was related to the area of a rectangle, two variables are initialized, h and b, these variables need that we enter the value of the height and base, then, these variables will be transformed to integers by means of the function int().

Subsequently, and having the variables as integers, we proceed to enter into the conditional block and thus to calculate the required area. Firstly, we see the condition, in this case, has to be satisfied, so much that the number that relates to the base and the number that relates to the height, are positive, but simultaneously. If this condition is true, we proceed to calculate the area, we initialize a variable that has the value of the multiplication of the other two variables, and finally, we convert it into a string, so we can make the print().

Now in the case that the condition has not been satisfied, it will be shown in the screen a string that will say "Error" in order to make it clear that an error has happened in the program.

Finally, to finish the program, a print is made, which will inform us that the program has finished and that will print a "Bye" on the screen.

On the other hand, if we get to make the example of the division, this would be very similar to what we have just done, since the else would also make a print of "Error" and also the condition of the if, will be equal to what was done in that example, because what has to be met that the denominator will be different from zero.

CHAPTER 10:

OOP (Object-Oriented Programming)

O bject-oriented programming is a form of programming in which we can observe in a more real way than the things that occur to us at the time of programming. This is a paradigm, which refers to theories, models, and methods that allow us to solve more quickly and efficiently any problem that may arise.

As its name implies, object-oriented programming is based on the object model, where the object itself is the main element that will contain all its characteristics and behavior, making it independent, but at the same time relating it to elements of a class.

This type of programming differs from structured programming since its main objective is that through some input data, produce an output.

Some of the benefits of working with OOP are:

- We can maintain a certain uniformity in the code.
- It allows the reuse of code, since it allows us, after having created an object, to use that same definition, to create other objects.
- It is a good practice when it comes to programs, not to say that it is one of the big pros of Python.

As we have seen before, object-oriented programming is a way of programming based on finding a solution to problems. This type of programming introduces new concepts, which complement and even overcome those we already know. But first, we should ask ourselves:

What Is a Class?

It is the way we can begin to create our own objects, since from there, we can add to each class its attributes that are nothing more than that class and its methods, which are something like the actions that the class can perform.

A clear example, to understand this, is that we have the computer class, which can have a mark, a color, a RAM memory, a ROM memory, a processor, among other things, being these the attributes of our class; then there are the actions that computers can do, such as navigate, turn on, turn off, sound, among others, being this the methods of our class.

In order to create a class, in this case, that of computers, let's see the following example:

```
classexample.py ×

1    class PC():
2        manufacturer="Dell"
3        ram="4 Gb"
4        rom="512 Gb"
5        processor="Intel I5"
6
```

As we can see in this example, we created the PC class, the brand is Dell, has 4 Gb of RAM, 512 Gb of ROM and an Intel i5 processor; this is the way we can create a class that only has attributes, but to make use of this class, we need to create an object, which will be explained below.

Object characteristics:

- **Object:** An object is an instance of a class. This entity is the result of a set of properties, attributes, behaviour, or functionalities in which they react to events that occur in the program.

- **Method:** A method is a type of algorithm, which will be related to an object or its class itself. The execution of an algorithm is triggered after receiving a message which indicates what an object can do, and even the method itself can generate changes between its properties.

- **Message:** We define a message as the direct communication to the object, this one is going to order itself to execute some of its methods with the parameters that it contains associated, according to be the event that generates it.

- **Behaviour:** This will be defined by the messages or methods to which the object will know how to respond. What do we mean by this? This is nothing more than saying that the behaviour will be the operations that can be performed with the object.

- **Event:** We define an event as an event that occurs in our program, either interaction of the user with the computer or a message sent by an object. Our program takes control of the event through a message to the target. How is this? In a few words, we can say that an event is a reaction that triggers the behaviour of an object.

- **Attributes:** We define an attribute as the characteristic that a class is going to have.

- **Components of an object:** Objects are made up of attributes, identity, relationship, and methods.

- **Identification of an object:** an object is identified through a table that is going to be composed by the attributes and functions that correspond to it.

After having explained some characteristics of the objects, we can create our first object, in this case, our first computer:

```python
class PC():
    manufacturer="Dell"
    ram="4 Gb"
    rom="512 Gb"
    processor="Intel I5"

myPC=PC()
print(myPC.ram)
```

As we could see in this example, specifically in the past one, we created the class, as we did previously, then we created our first object, with the myopic name, which is of the PC type. To verify that the RAM of our computer is four gigabytes of RAM, we use the dot property.

This property is used to access the attributes of our objects, and this is done by placing a dot, as previously seen, and then write some attribute of the object.

But this sounds a little repetitive since it seems that all computers are the same, but Python had already thought about this, for it, there are constructors so that we can make objects as the user wants and not in a predetermined way. In the following example, we are going to place constructors and methods in the same example, with the objective of making a complete example so that it is clear to the readers:

```python
class PC():
    def __init__(self, manufacturer, ram, rom, processor):
        self.manufacturer= manufacturer
        self.ram=ram
        self.rom=rom
        self.processor=processor
        self.state=False

    def turnOn(self):
        self.state=True
        print("The PC is on")

    def TurnOff(self):
        self.state=False
        print("The PC is off")

myNewPC=PC("Accer", "8 Gb", "1 Tb", "AMD")
myNewPC.turnOn()
print(myNewPC.processor)
```

In this example, we can see how to create a class, since it has its respective constructor, which uses the reserved word self, which is used to access an attribute from any method without any inconvenience, also to observe how the other modules were created, you could realize that they have been created using as arguments the word self, no matter what method it is, that word should always be there, and also, every time you want to access an attribute within the class, it is necessary to use the word self, you could also see how we added the behaviour of turning the computer on and off.

The next act was to create an object called myNewPC, which is class PC, and also has the characteristics, whose brand is Acer, has 8 Gb of RAM, 1 Tb of ROM, and has an AMD processor. The next act was to turn on the pc, using the turnOn() method, using the methodology of the dot, and finally, we want to know which processor has our new computer, also using the nomenclature of the dot.

Already seeing the potentiality that this object-oriented programming has, we will be able to observe some very important properties of them:

- **Abstraction:** They enhance the most significant characteristics of each object in an analogy way that captures the behaviour of it. These objects present a degree of abstraction since they allow them to communicate with other objects of the same class even without needing to show their characteristics. Therefore, abstraction refers to an object being able to isolate itself from all others and only concentrate on its tasks.

- **Encapsulation:** This is based on bringing together all the elements that are considered of the same essence that contains the same level of abstraction in order to make a better design of the structure of the components of the system.

- **Polymorphism:** It is about the different methods or better said, behaviors associated with different objects that have the same name, because when the method is called, it will perform the behaviour corresponding to the object that is required; an example of this, can be that a car is going to start, being this the method, then we also have that a motorcycle can start, being this a method of this class too.

- **Modularity:** It responsible of dividing the program or the application in several stages, in this case, the modules; you can imagine it as an old equipment of diskettes, that the modules acted independently, where each one becomes independent modules of the others, allowing this way to run separately, but even so, these have connections with the other modules, but they do not depend on others to run, but that they could use the data of the other pieces of code.

- **Inheritance:** This characteristic is very important, since it relates to several classes, so that they relate between them, generating a type of hierarchy, so to speak, the objects that have less hierarchy are going to inherit properties and attributes of the classes that have a greater hierarchy. In this way, polymorphism and encapsulation can be organized and facilitated, thus allowing objects with a smaller hierarchy to be created and defined as more specialized objects of the higher classes. Therefore, a small example could be that a computer being a fathering class, and a daughter could be a telephone, inheriting all the properties of the father class, with others a little more specific.

Now, in the case that an object inherits more than one class, this object has greater complexity, being a very specific instance.

- **Creating a class daughter:** Already knowing the theory, we can see the following example, where we create a cell class because as we all know all modern cell phones are computers, but not all computers are cell phones, so let's see the following example:

As we could see in this example, a PC class is created, which we have seen previously how it was created, then we create the class daughter of

PC, it has a constructor and has as inputs, all the arguments of the father class, plus the arguments signal and battery; then to initialize the constructor, we call the method of the father class __init__(), and then we will initialize the other two attributes as it is normally done, assigning to it the value of self.signal and self.battery, the corresponding values.

It also creates a call () method for the phone to call, and this method will show a message which will say that the phone is calling.

To instantiate a daughter class, what we do is to write a variable, which will be cell phone class, we insert the different arguments, such as Huawei brand, ARM processor, among other features. Then we will call the call () method so that our cell phone calls, and finally, we want to visualize which is the brand of our phone.

CHAPTER 11:

Preparing Your Self for Coding

Another fun thing to work with when you are in the conditional statements, these are going to be known by a lot of different names, such as "if" statements and the decision control statements. But they are going to be a great option when you would like the program to learn how to do a few things on its own, without you having to think about all of the possible inputs before you even start. There are going to be times when you would like to make sure that your code behaves in the right manner and can make some decisions on its own when you are not able to be there to monitor it all and hope that it all fits into the right place. Any time that you have a part of your code that will allow the user to put in any kind of answer that they want all on their own, rather than just selecting from a few options, then you are going to find that the conditional statements are the best ones to work with.

In this phase, we are going to take a look at the three most common options of the conditional statements that you are likely to use with some of your coding. The three that we are going to focus on the most are the "if" statement, the if-else statement, and the "elif" statement. These will all work in a slightly different manner from one another, but they can all add some great things to your code, so we are going to spend our time taking a look at them and how they are going to work for our needs.

The "If" Conditional Statements

The first thing we are going to look at is regular "if" statement. This keeps things simple and will ensure that we are set and ready to handle some of the basics of these conditional statements. This one is based on the idea that the answer the user gives is true or it is false, depending on what conditions you have set. If the user adds in input that the program is going to see as true, then your program will see this and will continue on to the next step. But if the user does put in an answer that is seen as false for that part of the code, then the program will just end because nothing is set up to handle this issue along the way. As we can see here already, there is the potential for some problems when you are working with this kind of coding. But we are still going to take a quick look at this to see how it works and to get the basic idea of these conditional statements, and then move on to how we can change things on to fix this issue. A good example of how the, if the statement is able to work, will be below:

age = int(input("Enter your age:")) if (age <=18):

print("You are not eligible for voting, try next election!")

print("Program ends")

Let's explore what is going to happen with this code when you put it into your program. If the user comes to the program and puts that they are younger than 18, then there will be a message that shows up on the screen. In this case, the message is going to say, "You are not eligible for voting, try next election!" Then the program, as it is, is going to end. But what will happen to this code if the user puts in some age that is 18 or above?

With the "if" statement, nothing will happen if the user says that their age is above 18. The "if" statement just has one option and will focus on whether the answer that the user provides is going to match up with the conditions that you set with your code. The user has to put in that they are under the age of 18 with the "if" statement in this situation, or you won't be able to get the program to happen again.

As we have already mentioned with this one, the "if" statement could end up causing us a few problems when we are coding. You want to make sure that the user is able to put in any answer that is the best for them, not the "right" answer, and you want to make sure that the program you are writing is still going to be able to respond and give some kind of answer to the user along the way. Some of the users who come to your website or program will have an age that is higher than 18, and it is going to be confusing and look bad if they put that answer in and can't get the program to work.

The If-Else Conditional Statement

This is why we are going to move on to the if-else statement. This one is used a lot more often than we see with the "if" statement, and it is able to handle some of the problems that we saw with the "if" statement. This kind of statement is going to work with some of the topics that we had above and make some changes to fix the issues and ensure that this all works.

Let's say that we are still working with the same kind of program that we had above. But this time, we want to make sure that we have some kind of result show up on the screen, no matter what answer the user inputs into our program this time. So, with this one, we are going to work to separate out the users based on their age. There will be a group that is above 18 and one that is under 18, and a response from the system based on this. The code that we would be able to use to help us write out our own "if else" statement is going to be below:

age = int(input("Enter your age:")) if (age <=18):

print("You are not eligible for voting, try next election!")

else print("Congratulations! You are eligible to vote. Check out your
        local

polling station to find out more information!) print("Program ends")

As you can see, this really helps to add some more options to your code and will ensure that you get an answer no matter what results the user gives to you. You can also change up the message to say anything that you want, but the same idea will be used no matter the answer that the user gives. You have the option to add in some more possibilities to this. You are not limited to just two options, as we have above. If this works for your program, that is just fine to use. But if you need to use more than these two options, you can expand out this as well. For example, take the option above and expand it to have several different age groups. Maybe you want to have different options come for those who are under 18, those that are between the ages of 18 and 30, and those who are over the age of 30. You can separate it out in that way, and when the program gets the answer from the user, it will execute the part that you want. The cool thing with this is there are a lot of different options and programs that we are able to write that work with this. Maybe we want to create our own program that allows the user to go through and pick out one of their favorite types of candy. There are a ton of different types of candy, and they go by so many different names that it is really hard to list them all out and be prepared for this ahead of time. But the "if else" statement would be able to help us to handle all of this.

With this one, we would just pick out a certain number of candy choices that we would like, maybe the top six, and then list out a response that goes with that. And then, we would use "if else" statement at the end in order to catch all of the answers that did not fit in with the original six that we listed out. This ensures that no matter what input the user adds to the system, they are going to get some kind of response out of the process as well. The else statement in all of this is going to be an important thing to make sure it is there because it is responsible for catching all of the answers that are left that the user could potentially give to you. If you don't have this statement placed in the code, or not in the right part of the code, it is not going to be able to catch all of the other possible inputs of the user as you would like.

Now that we have had a chance to talk about the "if" statement and the "if else" statement, it is time for us to move on to our "elif" statements. These are a unique part of programming in the Python language, and they are going to help us add in another level to some of the conditional statements that we are able to work with. This kind of conditional statement is going to allow for a user to pick out a few choices that you present to them, and then, depending on what answer or choice the user goes with, the program is going to execute the code and provide the results that go with that answer.

The Elif Conditional Statement

You will find that these "elif" statements are going to show up in a lot of different places. One option is going to be when they show up in the games that you play. If you have ever gone through and played a game or been on another kind of program where you are given a menu style of choices to make, then you have already had some experience with these "elif" statements doing their work.

CHAPTER 12:

The Future of Machine Learning

Machine Learning has been one of the most exciting developments to come out of computer science and artificial intelligence in a very long time. Of course, Machine Learning began its long road to its present form many decades ago. But it's only recently that we've seen Machine Learning getting widespread application to the extent that it's actually changing the way that society is operating. Understanding these changes is going to be one of the most important things going forward for the data science community and society at large. I try to stay optimistic, there are some reasons for concern, but I have to keep believing that Machine Learning is going to provide many tools that are going to help improve people's lives. Every tool development Machine Learning doesn't have to be the most dramatic and breakthrough development of that man has ever seen. We can probably go through history, and I would have to say that people like Nicholas Tesla or Thomas Edison we're probably a lot more impactful on society than a lot of the new technologies that we see today. I would say that's the truth for any given individual technology. However, when you take a look at the sum total of the changes that we are seen from Machine Learning, society is going to be transformed a great deal in the coming decades.

One of the things that we are definitely going to see is there are going to be a great deal of jobs that are eliminated. We have already seen the development of robots that can stack and manage warehouse just as well as any human worker. They haven't yet been deployed in a real situation, but the fact is it's only a matter of time before that happens. Second, we've already seen the developments of robots that can do many menial labor jobs. The most famous of these is a robot which is able to cook hamburgers in a fast-food restaurant. This may be unfortunate for those pushing for a $15 an hour wage for that type of work because right now, the robot is too expensive to be practical. But if you keep pushing it at some point, the robot becomes a cost-effective investment. Regardless of what happens, regarding the wages, the downward pressure on costs that usually happens with technology almost ensures that robots that do menial labor are going to be taking a lot of jobs over the next 5 to 10 years.

Remember that this is nothing new, however. I hate to bring it up yet again, but people in the 18th Century had great fears of losing their jobs to the new machines that were then making their way throughout society. The concerns of those people turned out totally misguided. In fact, they were dead wrong. Of course, that doesn't mean that we should mock anyone who has concerns about these lost jobs now, nor does it mean that we should dismiss them. We can't assume that because jobs were created in much larger numbers in the past due to technological changes that this is always going to happen. However, if I have to been on it, I would definitely suggest that that's probably the case. One thing that people are really good at is finding new things to do. Look around you and observe all the things that we do now that were even existing as a mere thought 50 or a hundred years ago. As an example, consider the video game industry. Today it generates billions of dollars, and it employs tens of thousands of people. Every time that human labor is liberated, new uses for it are quickly found.

It's hard to say where the future Machine Learning lies, but one thing it's going to do is allow people to have a more personalized existence. We've already seen great strides towards this over the past decade or so. Now everything is personally curated from music to videos. This process is in their early stages of development. It's only going to accelerate in the coming decades.

Another thing we likely see, is the application of Machine Learning to more and more areas throughout life. The growth of data science and Machine Learning has been explosive in the past 10 to 15 years. That trend is likely to continue.

When I was in college one of my computer science professors what at the time seemed like a completely ridiculous proposal, he said that in the future you could eliminate the need for programmer. He did envision this system of black boxes where you built up a layer that reduced the complexity and moved away from having to talk directly to the computer, replacing it with something extremely simple that practically anybody could understand. So people will be able to program just by moving around objects on the screen and connecting them with lines. This dream is already being realized. One example is a product named build box. This is a simple example that you should check it out online to understand the power behind it. It's a tool that allows people to develop video games without using any programming whatsoever. The selling point of this product is that it eliminates the programmer. All you do is drag and drop objects on the screen like you are using PowerPoint or keynote. It's really something else. And while it is used primarily to develop mobile games, the general principles behind it can be used for any type of programming.

One very important factor which I will call the Ace in the hole is Quantum Computing. It's unclear at this point whether Quantum Computing is something that will become practical or remain in the realm of theoretical investigation. If practical and functional quantum computers are ever built it will be a game-changer on the scale of the Industrial Revolution. How Quantum Computing is merged with Machine Learning could be one of the most interesting intellectual challenges in the coming century. There is no question that if Quantum Computing becomes a practicality, life is going to be very different afterwards. The changes that we're experiencing right now are going to seem incredibly trivial.

Conclusion

This is the end of this book and, in turn, the end of your introduction to the basis of Coding. If you've followed keenly through the chapters and have understood the rules and basis of all that has been taught so far, then you can proudly declare that you know and understand an important computer language. Truth be told, all that you've been taught so far isn't all there is to computer programming. But it's all you need to learn to stand on your own and pick up what's left. Nobody ever knows all of the Coding totally at once, it's a very long learning process. It takes constant practice and consistency. Coding isn't a subject or course you try out and leave for a very long time without trying your hands at well except you've decided it really isn't for you. Let's highlight some of the things we've been able to discuss and learn so far. Why do you need to code your resources?

The coding of the content of your resources can contribute significantly to your analysis in several ways:

- Coding will generate the ideas while codifying the material of its resources. It is possible to interpret the passages and discover new meaning in data.

- Coding allows you to gather and view all the material related to a category or case through all its resources. Viewing all this material allows you to review the coded segments in context and create new and more refined categories as you gain a new understanding of the meaning of the data.

- The codification of its resources facilitates the search for patterns and theories. It is possible to browse the encoded content of your resources using queries and search functionality to test theories and find new patterns in your data.

Coding for Kids will spark their creative intuitiveness process and spark a skill that enables them to try and create similar or even better things.

Like learning a new language, it is important to utilize the brain of your children while they are still young and open to new information. It is a lot harder to start learning a new language with zero background when you are an adult.

Take note that Coding can be defined as the act of telling the computer what to do in a language that it can understand. The languages used to achieve this are called programming languages. And they include Python, JavaScript, C, C++, and many more.

And always remember that Coding is like writing a chapter, whereas programming is writing a book.

And programming involves deciding the right instructions and then providing instructions for a machine to carry it out, of course, with the expectation of a certain result, whereas coding is translating those predetermined instructions into a language the computer can understand.

As early as 7 years of age, your child will have developed enough cognitive and critical-thinking abilities that are required to learn how to code. By the time they are 10, they can create computer programs of high quality, and that is of a professional standard.

I hope you have learned something

PYTHON FOR KIDS

An Easy And Practice Guide For Beginners To Introduce Programming With Python

SEAN DAMON

Table of Contents

Introduction 212

Chapter 1: What Is Coding 215

Chapter 2: Installation And Running Of Python 221

Chapter 3: The Importance Of Data Types And Variables ... 226

Chapter 4: Strings, Lists, Dictionaries, And Tuples 233

Chapter 5: Python Modules 240

Chapter 6: Classes And Objects 248

Chapter 7: Idle 255

Chapter 8: Numbers And Operators 268

Chapter 9: Operators In Python 275

Chapter 10: Essential Libraries For Machine Learning In Python 281

Chapter 11: How Can Python Work With Machine Learning ... 292

Chapter 12: Machine Learning And Data Science 297

Chapter 13: Decision Trees 303

Conclusion 312

Introduction

C oding in Python is straightforward and promises a fun experience that beats basic routine programming. Below are some benefits of why Kids should start learning on how to code with Python:

Easier and Better Debugging

Debugging refers to a process of searching for bugs and defects and resolving them. These bugs and errors tend to inhibit a program or system from working correctly. In this vein, debugging aims to resolve problems in programs. In terms of debugging, Python is one of the highest-ranking programming languages owing to the tools it provides, such as PyDebug, pudb, and pdb, which help make the debugging experience smooth and manageable.

Take, for instance, the tool—pudb, can help programmers analyze the core of codes and track down a problem. When compared, while other languages keep working to improve their debugging experiences and tools, Python only gets better with time.

There Are No Restrictions to its Programming Syntax

Unlike other programming languages, Python can be easily understood by anyone, even up to a non-programmer. The reason is primarily attributed to its high readability and problem-oriented design, which lets one pay attention to coding logically rather than expressly delving into the nitty-gritty of the syntax.

As proof of this unique benefit, consider the sample program shown below to calculate a simple interest.

```
Print ('Simple Interest Calculator :')
Amount = float (input ('Value of Principal?'))
roe = float(input('Rate of Interest ?'))
time = int(input('Duration (no. of years) ?'))
total = (amount * pow(1 + (roi/100), time)
interest = total - amount
print('\nInterest = %0.2f' %interest)
```

Taking a look at the program, you can note how relatively easy it is to decode and write the code in Python.

An Explicit Declaration is not Required

When coding in Python, type specifiers should not be used in the declaration of variables because it can be done without declaring any of the data types in Python. Additionally, it is unnecessary to make use of separators, such as semicolons (;) in marking the end of a statement or command. Indentation in Python takes the place of parenthesis in grouping a block of code. And to make indentations in codes, you can make use of either spaces or tabs. Albeit, some rules are enforced in Python, like the use of four spaces for each level of indentation, many other facets of Python, such as this contribute to making learning easier for beginners.

Great Object-Oriented Programming Support

OOP (Object-Oriented Programming) comes as a built-in element in Python. It creates a model that produces solutions by devising objects, binding data, and defining connections. Albeit, the procedural programming methodology takes a different approach from top to bottom, solving one problem at once and splitting it into bit sizes. Object-Oriented Programming, on the one hand, is a different ball game altogether. It adopts a bottom to top problem-solving approach that looks for blueprints to the solution from the onset, thereby leaving implementation to a much later time.

To develop you as a professional Python programmer, constructing objects, building inheritance, and using classes are fundamental approaches to take. What's more, is that these concepts can be easily mastered in Python for the production of quality programs with quicker implementations than other programming languages. Python encourages minimalism in code sizes, allowing for faster and better applications.

CHAPTER 13:

What is Coding

When we talk about the word coding, we will quickly see that it is a vast and big world to look at. It is not going to include just one or two parts. It is going to include hundreds of languages, thousands of software programs, and so much more. For example, all of the software that you are going to use on your desktop and laptop, and even the games and the apps that you enjoy on your smartphone are all going to be products of this coding. Even if you are working with a gadget or a device that does not have a screen, such as an RC drone, or even the toy Furby, you will not be able to behave in the proper manner without some of the software that coders have been able to develop.

That is why we are going to get started on some of the different parts that are going to show up when it is time to work with the idea of coding and programming. No matter what kind of coding or programming language you are looking to get into, there are always a bunch of options, and figuring out how they all work, and the basics that they will all share, can make a difference in the amount of success you are going to see.

The first thing that we need to do is to explore the most common terms and the definitions that go with them in Coding. No matter what kind of code you would like to do, or the coding language that you want to choose, knowing these basics can be important. Some of the terms that you need to know to get started will include:

Program and Code

Code is going to refer to the set of instructions that you can write out for the computer, or your compiler, to follow. As soon as you made a new code on a computer, and you wrote it out in a manner that the computer can process from the beginning all the way to the end without an error, you can already compile it into the program that you want.

Each programming language is going to come with its own rules when it comes to how the code should be written, and how you will work with each part of the program. Just know for now that the code is going to be the instructions that you are able to send through to the compiler, telling it how you want that program to behave.

Algorithms

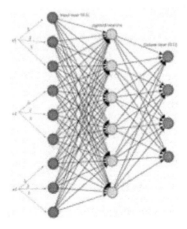

Even as a beginner, it is a good idea for you to learn a bit more about flowcharts and algorithms, even before you get really into some of the other complex stuff. When people code, they are working on providing a good solution to a problem, and they have to do this in a manner that the computer is able to understand. But if you spend too much of your time trying to craft each line of code without having a clear objective, you may find that you also have to spend a lot of time editing the code when you find out that the solution you came up with did not really address the problem, or at least not all of the situations of the problem.

Remember here that programs can be really complex to work with. According to Wired, in 2015, all of the services that Google provided over the internet were powered by 2 billion lines of code. Even some of the easier and more simple options that we would see with code, like the Windows 10 Calculator, comes with over 35,000 lines of code. Even with all of this coding, we have to remember that we can't get through all of this or make it work well if we don't go through with a game plan right from the beginning, and this is where the algorithms are going to come in to help.

The neat thing that you will notice about these algorithms is that you can do some work with them, even if you are not familiar with coding in the first place. You don't even need to work with a computer, though this does add an element of ease to the process. An algorithm is similar to what we are going to find with the code we talked about before, but it is going to be done in a manner that humans, not just the computer can understand, and it helps to give us a game plan of how to handle some of the more complex types of codes that we are going to work with.

Flowcharts

If this works, there should be some cookies that will come to your chosen website. You can then use the cookies that you have collected. You are able to use the information from the cookies, which should be saved to the website of your choice, for whatever purpose you need.

A good way for us to think about these flowcharts is as a graphical representation of an algorithm. Since these algorithms are simply just a translation of code into a human-friendly manner, a flowchart is going to provide us with more of a bird's eye view of the functionality of the code from start to finish. If you have ever done or even seen a flowchart to help see how the workflow should go, you will find that the flowcharts for coding work in a similar manner.

Flowcharting is useful in many cases because it is going to help us to make some of the more complicated programs that we need to handle significantly easier to understand. And it helps us to illustrate these complicated programs before we proceed through the coding, ensuring that we find the flaws that we want, and can make it so that we see additional features where they need to be. However, as a beginner, the best place to start is to learn about the five flowchart symbols that are going to be used in any coding flowchart that you want to work with. These are going to include:

Oval Start and End

The oval, or the ellipse, is going to be a symbol that will tell us the beginning and the end of the flow of the program. To make the flowchart stay as simple as we can, you need to only use two of these ovals one for the beginning and one for the end. You can go with more than this though if your program is designed to have more than one ending.

Arrow

This is going to be the line that we are able to use to help connect the shapes of your flowchart together, with the arrowhead being used to tell us which direction the flow of the program is going. This is used to help eliminate the need for putting in numbered steps like you need to do when making one of the algorithms from before. Arrows add in some flexibility to the flow of your chart and can cut down on some of the clutter when the program is more complicated.

Parallelogram Input and Output: This is going to help us to see the operation for the input or the output. Whenever you would like to accept a value from the user, which is the input, or you would like to display a value, which is the output, in your program, make sure that the parallelogram shows up.

Rectangle the process

This is going to help us to see any operation that is performed internally by the computer. Basically, any operation that is direct, that doesn't accept input or doesn't display an output needs to be represented with this rectangle. For example, calculations similar to the modular division can use this kind of symbol.

Rhombus Decision

This is going to be a symbol that will be used to help branch out the flow of the program or help out when handling conditional statements. It is still going to count as a process because the computer will internally do the operation, but it has to decide and then pick out the right path based on the condition that you set.

These symbols are going to be recognized universally by programmers and others who do coding, so make sure that when you are using one of these charts, you are also working with the right symbols along the way.

CHAPTER 14:

Installation and Running of Python

Official Version Installation

Mac

Python is already pre-installed on the Mac and can be used directly. If you want to use other versions of Python, we recommend using the Homebrew installation. Open the Terminal and enter the following command at a command-line prompt, which brings you to Python's Interactive Command Line:

$python

The Python input above is usually a soft link to a version of a Python command, such as version 3.5. If the corresponding version is already installed, you can run it in the following manner:

$python3.5

The terminal will display information about Python, such as its version number, followed by a command-line prompt for Python. If you want to exit Python, type:

>>>exit()

If you want to run a Python Program in your current directory, append the name to Python or Python 3:

$python installation.py

If the file is not in the current directory, you need to specify the full path of the file, such as:

$python/home/authorname/installation.py

We can also change the installation.py to an executable script. Just add the Python interpreter you want to use to the first line of the installation.py:

#!/usr/bin/env Python

In the terminal, change the installation.py to executable:

$chmod installation.py

Then, on the command line, type the name of the program file, and you're ready to run it using the specified interpreter:

$./installation.py

If the installation.py is in the default path, then the system can automatically search for the executable and run it in any path:

$installation.py

Linux

Linux systems are similar to MAC systems, and most come preloaded with Python. There are many Linux systems that offer something like Homebrew's software manager, which, for example, is installed under Ubuntu using the following command:

$sudo apt-get install Python

Under Linux, Python is used and run in much the same way as on the MAC, and I won't go into that again.

Windows Operating System

For the Windows operating system, you need to download the installation package from the official Python Website. If you don't have access to Python's website, search engines for keywords like "Python Windows download" to find other download sources. The installation process is similar to installing other Windows software. In the install screen, Customize the installation by selecting Customize, in addition to selecting Python components, check:

Add python.exe to Path

Once installed, you can open the Windows command line and use Python as you would on a Mac.

Other Python Versions

The official version of Python mainly provides compiler/interpreter functionality. Other unofficial versions have richer features and interfaces, such as a more user-friendly graphical interface, a text editor for Python, or an easier to use module management system for you to find a variety of extension modules. In unofficial Python, the two most commonly used are:

1) Anaconda

2) Thought Python Distribution (EPD)

Both versions are easier to install and use than the official version of Python. With the help of a module management system, programmers can also avoid annoying problems with module installation. So, it's highly recommended for beginners. Anaconda is free, and EPD is free for students and researchers. Because of the graphical interface provided, their use method is also quite intuitive. I strongly recommend that beginners choose one of these two versions to use. The exact usage can be found in the official documentation and will not be repeated here.

Virtualenv

You can install multiple versions of Python on a single computer, and using virtualenv creates a virtual environment for each version of Python. Here's how to install virtualenv using Python's included pip.

$pip install virtualenv

You can create a virtual space for a version of Python on your computer, such as:

$virtualenv –p /usr/bin/Python3.5 virtualPythonexample

In the above command, /usr/bin/Python3.5 is where the interpreter is located, and virtualPythonexample is the name of the newly created virtual environment.

The following command can start using the MYENV virtual environment:

$source virtualPythonexample/bin/activate

To exit the virtual environment, use the following command:
$deactivate

CHAPTER 15:

The Importance of Data Types and Variables

N

ow it is time for us to take a moment to look at some of the work that can be done with the data types and the variables that come with the Python language. Both of these are going to be important and will tell us a lot when it is time to work with the Python language as well. We are not going to get very far in some of the programmings that we want to do if we aren't able to learn some of the different types of data that are out there, and we aren't able to have a good understanding of how the variables work as well. Let's take a look at some of the different types of data that come with Python, and how these variables work, so we are able to put it all together and see some great results in the process.

The Python Data Types

The first thing that we need to focus on here is the data types that come with Python. Each of the values that we are going to work within Python is going to have a data type. Since everything in this programming language is going to be an object, the types of data are actually going to be classes, and then the variables are going to be instances, or objects, of these classes. This is how all of the work is going to be tied in together.

Now, you will find that there are various types of data that can show up in Python. Some of the ones that are the most important ones, and the ones that you are likely going to spend the majority of your time on in Python will be tackle below:

First on the list is the Python numbers. These are going to include floating-point numbers, complex numbers, and integers. These are going to be brought out with the help of the function of type (), which can help us to know which class a variable or our value is going to belong to. This helps us to make sure that we are able to pull out the numbers that we would like in this coding language.

We can also send out the Python list. This list is going to simply be an ordered sequence of items that we can work with. It is going to actually be the type of data that we are able to work within Python that is used the most, and it is very flexible. All of the items that are on the list do not need to end up being the same type of data either. In addition, the lists are going to be mutable, which simply means that the elements that are on the list can be altered in any way that you want.

The Python tuple is also going to be important. The tuple is going to be an ordered sequence of items just the same as we see with the list. The biggest difference that you are going to see with these tuples is that they are immutable. Once you create one of these tuples, you are not able to make modifications to them. Tuples are going to be there to help us write/protect the data, and are usually going to perform faster than a list because it is not going to change dynamically at all.

The Python string is the next thing that we are able to focus some attention on. The string is basically going to be a sequence of Unicode characters. We are going to have the option of working with either a single quote or a double quote to help represent strings. You can also work with some multi-line strings.

The Python set is going to be another type of data that we are able to work with, and it is basically a collection of items that are unique and will not be ordered. The set is going to be defined by values that are separated by a comma, and then these items are going to be inside of braces. Items in a set are not going to be ordered at all.

And finally, we are going to take a look at the Python dictionary. The dictionary is basically going to be an unordered collection of key-value pairs. This is the one that is generally going to be used when we have to handle a very large amount of data. Dictionaries are going to be optimized to help us retrieve the data we want. We also have to make sure that we know the key before the data is going to be available. With the Python language, we are going to be able to define these dictionaries within braces, with each item being a pair in the form of key: value. You are able to have the key and the value of any type that you would like.

The Python Variables

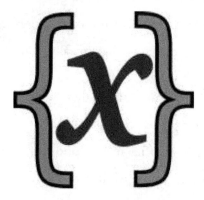

The next topic that we need to spend some time on in this guidebook is going to be the variables. The variables are basically anything that is able to hold onto a value or one of the data types that we talked about from before, that can change. Often we are able to think about these variables as a box that is capable hold onto the values that we are using in Python. These are important for us to focus on because they will save some space on our memory, and then allow us to pull that variable back out at a later time.

These variables are something that all programmers need to learn about because they will basically be saved spaces in the memory of the

229

computer, and then you are able to tell the computer that it is time to pull them out at any time when you are ready. The variables that you take the time to create are going to be found in certain locations in the memory of the system you are using, and then they can be found and executed when the code is running. Depending on the type of data that you would like to focus on, the variable is going to be the part that will tell the compiler where to save that information to make it available when needed.

One of the most important things that we need to focus on when it comes to working with these variables is making sure that we assign a value to it. If you do not assign one or more values to your variable, you are going to end up saving some empty space on your memory, and nothing is going to come up in the code when you pull it up. If the variable has some kind of value that has been assigned back to it, and sometimes it will have more than one value on it, then it is going to react in the manner that you would like in this code.

Any time that we are working on some of these variables, you will find that there are basically three main options that you are able to choose from for it. Each of these is going to be useful, and it is often going to depend on the codes you are trying to write, and the type of value that you are sending over to the variable. The options that you are able to pick from include:

- Float: this would include numbers like 3.14 and so on.

- String: this is going to be like a statement where you could write out something like "Thank you for visiting my page!" or another similar phrase.

- Whole number: this would be any of the other numbers that you would use that do not have a decimal point.

When you are working with variables in your code, you need to remember that you don't need to take the time to make a declaration to save up this spot in the memory. This is automatically going to happen once you assign a value over to the variable using the equal sign. If you want to check that this is going to happen, just look to see that you added that equal sign in, and everything is going to work.

Assigning a value over to your variable is pretty easy. Some examples of how you can do this in your code would include the following:

x = 12#this is an example of an integer assignment

pi = 3.14#this is an example of a floating-point assignment

customer name = John Doe this is an example of a string assignment

Another option that you can do here, and that we have mentioned a little bit in this phase already, is a variable assigned to two or more values. There are some instances when you are writing code, and you will need to take two values and place them with the same variable.

To make sure that you are able to go through this, we simply need to work with some of the same procedures that we talked about through this phase. We just need to make sure that we are putting in the equal signs in the right spots so that the compiler knows which values are going to the variable. So, you could write out something like a = b = c = 1 to show the compiler how each of these variables is going to equal 1. Or you could write out something like 1 = b = 2 to show that this variable is going to have two values assigned to it.

One of the most important things that we are able to focus on here is that the variable has to be assigned over to a value in order to work the way that we want in the code, and that these variables are basically just an empty spot in the memory that is reserved for the value that you decide to assign to the variable. Then, when it is time for the compiler to call up some of these values, it is going to be able to call up the variable, and all of it is going to show up the way that you want.

There are many times when you will need to work with these variables in your code, and they are often going to be assigned with some of the types of data that we were talking about earlier in this phase. When we are able to make all of these parts fit in with one another, we will find that it is so much easier for us to get the results that we would like in the process. Make sure to learn about these variables, and how to properly set it up with the right value in order to get the code to work the way that you would like.

CHAPTER 16:

Strings, Lists, Dictionaries, and Tuples

P rogrammers often use strings, lists, dictionaries, and tuples when they write a script in Python. These data types are known as data structures. Strings are pieces of text that are grouped, while tuples and lists are groups of individual data items that have been grouped. A dictionary is a group of pairs that have the highest considerations. The different methods that are used to access the data in these structures are the same.

You can also look at these data types differently, depending on whether the values that the variable holds can be modified. This is called the mutability of the data type. A string and tuple cannot be modified, but they can be used to create new tuples and strings. A list is mutable, which means that you can either remove or add items to it.

Items in Sequences

You can fetch individual items in a sequence using an index. This index will indicate the position of the element. The index is often an integer that is written in square brackets immediately after the name of the variable. So, you can obtain the variable in a list by specifying the name of the list, followed by the index. You can also access a single character in a string.

>>> vegetable = 'pumpkin'

>>> vegetable [0]

'p'

Or an item in a list:

>>>vegetable = ['pumpkins', 'potatoes', 'onions', 'eggplant']

>>>vegetable [1]

'Pumpkins'

You will notice that indexing in Python is zero-based. This means that you can only start counting the variables at zero. An index with the number 3 in the square brackets will look at the fourth item in the list since the first item will be indexed as zero. So, you can use any number of integers beginning from zero to index the variables in your data set. A negative index will count the list from the end to the beginning:

>>>vegetable [-1]

'eggplant'

Slices can be used to grab the different sections in any sequence. This method is used to fetch many items in a sequence. A slice is written using the same notation as an index, the only difference is that a colon separates the integers. The first value is the starting point, and this value is included. The second number in the notation is the endpoint of the slice, and it is exclusive. If you look at s[0:2], the compiler will slice the list from the variable with the index zero and stop exactly before the variable with the index two. You do not necessarily have to use the third value, and this is an additional step. This can be negative; therefore, you can retrieve all the other items instead of picking this item from the sequential list. Alternatively, you can retrieve items backward as well. So, s [i: j: step] will give you the slice that begins from the variable i, but will not include the variable j. Here, s is the sequence.

If you ignore the initial point, the slice will always start at the beginning of the sequence. If you forget the end, the slice will continue to the end of the original or main sequence. Slicing and indexing do not change the original sequence, they will develop a new sequence. The actual data items in the sequence will be the same. So, if you want to modify an individual item in the sequence, you will see that the item has changed in the slice as well.

Tuples

Tuples are a group of items or elements that are ordered and immutable. You should think of a tuple as a sealed packet of information.

A tuple is specified as a comma-separated list of values. These values can be enclosed within parentheses if necessary. In some cases, these parentheses are required, so always use them regardless of whether or not you think they are necessary. The values in the tuple do not necessarily have to be of the same data type. Some values can also be other tuples.

Creating a Tuple

Tuples can be created with no items in it using the round brackets ().

>>>empty_tuple= ()

If you do not want more than one item in the tuple, you should enter the first item, followed by a comma.

>>>one_item = ('blue',)

Changing Values in a Tuple

The values in a tuple cannot be changed. These tuples are sealed packets of information that are often used in situations where a set of values need to be passed on from one location to another. If you wish to change the sequence of the data, you should use a list.

List

A list is a comma-separated and ordered list of items that are enclosed within square brackets. The items within the list do not have to be of the same data type. You can also include a list within a list.

A list can be concatenated, indexed, and sliced just like any other sequence you can use in Python. You can change some items within a list when compared to a tuple or string. Lists are very flexible when compared to tuples. You can either clear a list or change the list completely by slicing the list and assigning the data to other variables.

Creating a List

It is easy to create a list.

```
>>> shopping_list = ['detergent', 'deodorant', 'shampoo', 'body wash']
```

Modifying a List

A new value can be added to a list using the assignment operator.

```
>>> shopping_list [1] = 'candles'

>>> shopping_list
```

['detergent,' 'candles,' 'deodorant,' 'shampoo,' 'body wash']

Stacks and Queues

You can use lists to store and retrieve data or variables in a specific order since lists are ordered data types. The main models that one can use to do this are by using stacks and queues. A stack uses the last in first out (LIFO) approach. A real-world example of this approach is how the discard pile is used in a card game. You add cards to the top of the pile and remove the card from the top. You can include items into a stack using the list.append() function and remove the items from a stack using the pop() function. There are no additional index arguments that you will need to include when you use these functions, so the last item in the list is removed.

>>> shopping_list.append ('brush')

>>> shopping_list.pop()

'candles'

>>> shopping_list

['detergent,' 'deodorant,' 'shampoo,' 'body wash']

The second approach is to create the first in first out (FIFO) structure. A queue uses this type of approach. This method works like a pipe where the first item is pushed out of the pipe before the remaining items. You can use the same functions, append() and pop(), to either push items into the queue or remove them from the queue. You will, however, need to use the index zero to indicate that the items should be popped from the start of the list.

>>> shopping_list.append ('brush')

>>> shopping_list.pop(0)

'detergent'

>>> shopping_list

['deodorant,' 'shampoo,' 'body wash,' 'brush]'

Dictionaries

A dictionary is much like an address book. If you know the name of the person you wish to contact, you can obtain the details of that person. The name of the person is the key, while the details of the person are the value.

The key that you use in a dictionary should be an immutable data type; that is, it can be a number, tuple, or string. The value can be anything. A dictionary is a mutable data type, and it is for this reason that you can add, modify, or remove any pairs from the dictionary. The keys are mapped to an object, and it is for this reason that a dictionary is also known as mappings. This will show you that a dictionary behaves different to a sequence.

A dictionary can be used anywhere you want to store a value or attribute that will describe an entity or a concept. For instance, you can use a dictionary to count the number of instances of a specific state or object. Since every key has a unique identifier, you cannot have duplicate values for the same key. Therefore, the key can be used to store the items in the input data, and the values can store the result of the calculation.

CHAPTER 17:

Python Modules

Modules, also known as packages, are a set of names. This is usually a library of functions/object classes that are made available to be used within different programs. We used the notion of modules earlier in this phase to use some function from the math library. In this phase, we are going to cover in-depth on how to develop and define modules. To use modules in a Python program, the following statements are used: import, from, reload. The first one imports the whole module. The second allows import only a specific name or element from the module. The third one, reload, allows reloading a code of a module while Python is running and without stopping in it. Before digging into their definition and development, let's start first by the utility of modules or packages within Python.

Modules Concept and Utility Within Python

Modules are a very simple way to make a system component organized. Modules allow reusing the same code over and over. So far, we were working in a Python interactive session. Every code we have written and tested is lost once we exit the interactive session. Modules are saved in files that make them persistent, reusable, and sharable. You can consider modules as a set of files where you can define functions, names, data objects, attributes, and so on. Modules are a tool to group several components of a system in a single place. In Python programming, modules are among the highest-level unit. They point to the name of packages and tools. Besides, they allow the sharing of the implemented data. You only need one copy of the module to be able to use across a large program. If an object is to be used in different functions and programs, coding it as a module allows to share it with other programmers.

To have a sense of the architecture of Python coding, we go through some general structure explanation. We have been using so far in this book very simple code examples that do not have high-level structure. In large applications, a program is a set of several Python files. By Python files, we mean files that contain Python code and have a .py extension. There is one main high-level program, and the other files are the modules. The high-level file consists of the main code that dictates the control flow and executes the application. Module files define the tools that are needed to process elements and components of the main program and maybe elsewhere. The main program makes use of the tools that are specified in the modules.

In their turn, modules make use of tools that are specified in other modules. When you import a module in Python, you have access to every tool that is declared or defined in that specific module. Attributes are the variables or the functions associated with the tools within a module. Hence, when a module is imported, we have access to the attributes of the tools as well to process them. For instance, let's

241

consider we have two Python files named file1.py and file2.py, where the file1.py is the main program, and file2.py is the module. In the file2.py, we have a code that defines the following function:

```
def Xfactorial (X):

P = 1

for i in range (1, X + 1):

P *= i

return P
```

To use this function in the main program, we should define code statements in the file1.py as follows:

```
Import file2

A = file2.Xfactorial (3)
```

The first line imports the module file2.py. This statement means to load the file file2.py. This gives access to the file1.py to all tools and functions defined in file2.py by the name file2. The function Xfactorial is called by the second line. The module file2.py is where this function is defined using the attributes' syntax. The line file2.Xfactorial() means fetch any name value of Xfactorial and lies within the code body of file2. In this example, it is a function that is callable. So, we have provided an input argument and assigned the output result to the variable A. If we add a third statement to print the variable A and run the file file1.py, it would display 6 which is the factorial of 3. Along with Python, you will see the attribute syntax as object.attribute. This allows calling the attributes that might be a function or data object that provides properties of the object.

Note that some modules that you might import when programming with Python are available in Python itself. As we have mentioned at the beginning of this book, Python comes with a large stand library that has built-in modules. These modules support all common tasks that might be needed in programming from operating system interfaces to graphical user interface. They are not part of the language. However, they can be imported and comes with a software installation package. You can check the complete list of available modules in a manual that comes with the installation or goes to the official Python website: www.Python.org. This manual is kept updated every time a new version of Python is released.

How to Import a Module

We have talked about importing a module without really explaining what happens behind in Python. Imports are a very fundamental concept in Python programming structure. In this phase, we are going to cover in-depth how really Python imports modules within a program. Python follows three steps to import a file or a module within the work environment of a program. The first step consists of finding the file that contains the module. The second step consists of compiling the module to a byte-code if required. Finally, the third step runs the code within the module file to build the objects that are defined. These three steps are run only when the module is imported for the first time during the execution of a program. This module and all its objects are loaded in the memory. When the module is imported further in the program, it skips all three steps and just fetch the objects defined by the module and are saved in memory.

At the very first step of importing a module, Python has to find the module file location. Note that, so far in the examples we presented, we used import without providing the complete path of the module or extension .py. We just used import math, or import file2.py. Python import statement omits the extension and the path, we just simply import a module by its name. The reason for this is that Python has a module that looks for paths called 'search path module.' This module is used specifically to find the path of module files that are imported by the import statements.

In some cases, you might need to configure the path search of modules to be able to use new modules that are not part of the standard library. You need to customize it to include these new modules. The search path is simply the concatenation of the home directory, directories of PYTHONPATH, directories of the standard library, and optionally if the content of files with extension .pth when they exist. The home directory is set automatically by the system to a directory of Python executable when launched from the interactive session, or it can be modified to the working directory where your program is saved. This directory is the first to be searched when import a module is run without a path. Hence, if your home directory points to a directory that includes your program along with the modules, importing these modules does not require any path specification.

The directory of the standard library is also searched automatically. This directory contains all default libraries that come with Python. The directories of PYTHONPATH can be set to point toward the directory of new modules that are developed. In fact, PTYHONPATH is an environment variable that contains a list of directories that contains Python files. When PTYHONPATH is set, all these paths are included in the Python environment, and the search path directory would search these directories too when importing modules. Python also allows defining a file with .pth extension that contains directories, one in each line. This file serves the same as PTYHONPATH when included appropriately in a directory. You can check the directories' paths included when you run Python using sys.path. You simply print sys.path to get the list of the directories that Python will be searching for.

Remember, when importing a module, we just use the name of the module without its extension. When Python is searching for a module in its environment paths, it selects the first name that matches the module name regardless of the extension. Because Python allows using packages that are coded in other languages, it does not simply select a module with .py extension but a file name or even a zip file name that matches the module name being imported. Therefore, you should name your modules distinctly and configure the search path in a manner that makes it obvious to choose a module.

When Python finds the source code of the module file with a name that corresponds to the name in the import statement, it will compile it into byte code in case it is required. This step is skipped if Python finds an already byte code file with no source code. If the source code has been modified, another byte code file is automatically regenerated by Python while the program runs in other further executions. Byte code files have typically .pyc extension. When Python is searching and finds the module file name, it will load the byte code file that corresponds to the latest version of the source code with .py extension. If the source code is newer than the byte code file, it will generate a new one by compiling the source code file. Note that only imported files have corresponding files with .pyc extension. These files, the byte code files, are stored on your machine to make the imports faster in future use.

The third step of the import statement is running the module's byte code. Each statement and each assignment in the file are executed. This allows generating any function, data objects, and so on defined in the module. The functions and all attributes are accessed within the program via importers. During this step, you will see print statements if they exist. The 'def ' statement will create a function object to be used in the main program.

To summarize the import statement, it involves searching for the file, compiling it, and running the byte code file. All other import statements use the module stored in memory and ignore all the three steps. When first imported, Python will look in the search path module to select the module. Hence, it is important to configure correctly the path environment variable to point to the directory that contains new defined modules. Now that you have the big picture and the concept of modules, let's explore how we can define and develop new modules.

CHAPTER 18:

Classes and Objects

The Python Classes

The next thing that we need to focus on in the Python language is the classes. There is a lot that we are able to focus on when it comes to the Python classes, and knowing how to make this work is going to be so important to the work that you do in Python. Classes, to keep things as simple as possible, are going to be a type of container that can hold onto your objects, as well as some other parts of your code. You have to make sure that these classes are always named in the proper manner, and that you store them in the right spots to ensure they are able to work the way that you want. Then, we have to double-check that we are storing the right objects into these classes as well.

The neat thing here is that it is possible to take any object and put it into one of the classes that you choose to design. But there are a few rules. First, we have to make sure that the objects that are similar to one another end up in the same class.

Of course, you are not required to put the identical items in each class, but when you take a look at any class in your code, there has to be some sense as to why those items are in there together.

For example, you can create a class that will hold onto all types of vehicles, and it is not required that you fill it with just blue cars. You can mix and match the items or the objects in your classes, just make sure that the items and objects that are in a particular class make sense to be in there with one another, rather than just being random.

There are a lot of things that you are able to do with some of the classes that you are going to work on, but we are going to keep our focus on some of the steps that you can take in order to create one of these new classes. Because of the way that the Python language is set up, you will need to create a lot of classes in order to keep the information as organized as possible.

In Python, it is very important that we are able to spend our time working on creating some of our classes because this is one of the best ways for the code to be organized and to make sure that nothing is going to get lost in the process.

To make one of these classes on your own, though, you have to use the right keywords to name that class. You have some freedom here in naming the class, just make sure that the name you want to work with comes right after the keyword, and that it is a name that you will be able to remember at a later time.

After you have had a chance to name your class, it is time to work on naming the subclass that you are working with. This subclass is going to end up in the parenthesis if you would like to maintain some of the programming rules that we have in place. Make sure that at the end of the first line, when you are creating a new class, that there is a semicolon in place. While your code will technically work if you forget to add in this part, it is considered part of the coding rules to have this and will look a lot better if you make sure that it is there.

Writing a class right now probably sounds pretty confusing, and you may be worried that you won't be able to figure out how to make it happen, or how to get it to work for you. This is actually a fairly simple process and will not take up as much time and effort as you would like. To help us make this as easy as possible, let's take a break here and discuss the coding that is needed to write a class and how it is meant to look. If you would like to create one of your own classes, then the following code is the right one for you:

class Vehicle(object):

#constructor

def_init_(self, steering, wheels, clutch, breaks, gears):

self._steering = steering

self._wheels = wheels

self._clutch = clutch

self._breaks =breaks

```python
        self._gears  = gears

        #destructor

        def_del_(self):

            print("This is destructor....")

        #member functions or methods

        def Display_Vehicle(self):

            print('Steering:' , self._steering)

            print('Wheels:', self._wheels)

            print('Clutch:', self._clutch)

            print('Breaks:', self._breaks)

            print('Gears:', self._gears)

    #instantiate a vehicle option

    myGenericVehicle = Vehicle('Power Steering', 4, 'Super Clutch', 'Disk
    Breaks', 5)

    myGenericVehicle.Display_Vehicle()
```

If you would like, you can try out this code. Just open up your text editor and type the code inside. Once you have a chance to write out and then execute this code, let's divide it up and see what happened above.

The Python Objects

Now that we have taken a look at the Python classes, we need to take a look at some of the Python objects as well. The classes are going to be like the containers in this language, and then the objects are going to be the parts that we put into the containers to keep them nice and safe. This works because Python is considered an OOP language, or Object-Oriented Programming language.

That is why we are going to take a bit of time here to look at what this means for your coding, and why it is such an important part to include in some of our coding as well.

One of the features that programmers, especially those who are new to programming, will enjoy when it comes to using an OOP language is that the procedures of any object you use will have the power needed to access data fields, and there are even some situations where the objects are even able to modify these data fields. With this kind of language, we are able to create the kind of program that does this simply by building it from a series of objects that are capable of not only interact, but also talk with one another.

This may seem like a simplistic way to look at the whole process, but it helps us to get a better understanding of how this process works and how we are able to use it. You will find though that even with some of this simplicity, the idea that Python is an OOP language adds in some diversity to the process. Each language is going to come in with some differences, but the ones that you may use, including Python, are going to be known as class-based.

This means that the code is going to have each of the objects fall into a class of some sort, which is one of the best ways to make sure that all of this is as organized as possible.

As you start with some of the coding that is needed with Python, you will find that the fact that Python is an OOP language is going to be to your benefit. It can help make the writing of code easier than ever, and will ensure that it is going to make coding easy even if you are a beginner. This is especially true when we consider how hard it is to work with some of the older languages that are not going to be considered OOP.

Before we go further into OOP languages and what they mean, we need to do a quick summary of classes and how they work. Classes are like small containers. You can pick any name that you want for the classes and then add in any item that you would like. Of course, to keep things organized and to help you call up these classes later on in your code, it may be a good idea to pick out a name that describes what is held inside.

When you work on your objects in the code, you will find that they actually match up with real things outside of the programming world. For example, one of your objects might be a car, one might be a book, and one might be a ball. You also have the option of picking out an object that is a bit more abstract but sticks with things that work in the code that you are creating. These objects are going to stay inside any of the classes that you create and then place the object of sin. You want to make sure that any object that is inside the same class has some kind of similarities to each other. These objects don't have to be exactly alike. But if another programmer comes to look at the code, they should be able to figure out why one group of objects is placed in the same class.

An example of this would be a class with dogs inside. You don't have to just put St. Bernard's in the class unless you want to. You could include big dogs, small dogs, medium dogs, fluffy dogs, or any other kind of dog that you would like to put into this class. Other programmers will see that the objects aren't identical, but they will understand that your class is for dogs, rather than a specific type of dog.

These objects, as well as the classes that come with them, will be able to work with one another because they will make sure that the code you do in Python as neat and organized as they can. You are able to spend some time putting the objects that you have into the right class, which is going to keep things organized and allows your code to work in a more efficient manner. Even as a beginner, you will notice how much easier than the whole coding process can be when you want to keep things working efficiently with the Python language.

CHAPTER 19:

IDLE

When you download and install Python, it will also install an application called IDLE. Integrated Development and Learning Environment or also known as IDLE, it is an integrated development environment, or IDE, that helps us with writing Python programs.

Think of it as an electronic notepad with some additional tools to help us write, debug, and run our Python code.

To work in Python, you will need to open IDLE because opening Python files directly won't work!

On a PC

Step 1. Click the Windows Start menu.

Step 2. Start typing "idle", then select the search result IDLE (Python 3.7 64-bit). Note: Yours might say IDLE (Python 3.7 32-bit) if that's the kind of machine you have.

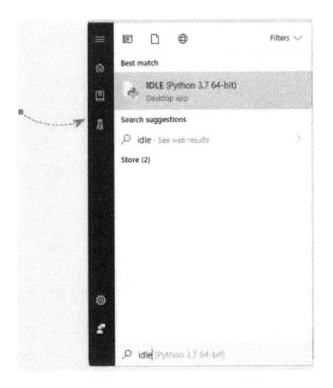

Step 3. A window should pop up that looks like this:

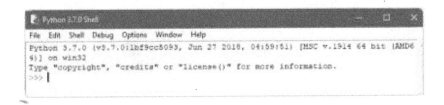

Step 4. Nice! You opened IDLE on Windows and are now ready to start writing some codes in Python!

On a Mac

Step 1. Navigate to GO > APPLICATIONS.

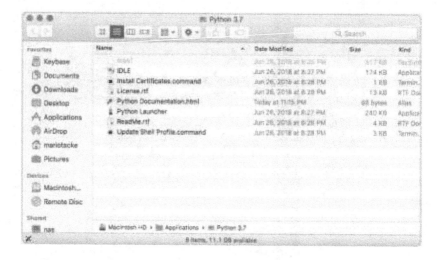

Step 2. Find the Python 3.7 folder and open it.

Step 3. Double-click on the IDLE icon.

Step 4. A window should pop up that looks like this:

```
Python 3.7.0 Shell
Python 3.7.0 (v3.7.0:1bf9cc5093, Jun 26 2018, 23:26:24)
[Clang 6.0 (clang-600.0.57)] on darwin
Type "copyright", "credits" or "license()" for more information.
>>>
```

Step 5. Congratulations! You opened IDLE on a Mac and are now ready to start writing some code in Python!

Python IDLE has the following features:

- Syntax highlighting

- Auto-completion of code statements

- Smart indentation
- Integrated debugger with the stepping, persistent breakpoints, and call stack visibility features.

Launching Python

To get started, you have to understand how to launch the Python app. You can launch Python from the Terminal or use the desktop environment for starting the IDLE app. Simply launch the Terminal and type: "idle" at the command prompt. Now that you've launched the Python, it's now time to begin coding.

Let's now create our first program in Python. Follow these steps to write your first Python program:

- Open the Python IDLE.
- Write the Python language statements (instructions) in the IDLE window.
- Run the program

That's it! Simple. Isn't it?

Now, here's a quick way to see the programming process in action...Proceed and copy/paste the following code into your Python IDLE window.

print ("Hello World! This is my first Machine Learning program")

Run the program. What do you see as the output?

Well, the phrase "Hello World! This is my first Machine Learning program" appears.

Congratulations! You've just written your first Python code. I know you're now excited to begin coding ML systems. Don't worry so much about the meaning of statements. If you are a Machine Learning novice, mastering some Python programming concepts will help you understand how to design ML applications.

Next up, let's dive in together and get to the basics of Python programming.

An Overview of Python

Now that you have executed your first Python program, what else do you need to know? Well, it's now time to understand the vital components of any Python code, including its structure. All Python programs have the following structure:

```
import sys

def main ():

main ()

{
```

Program statements

}

As you can see from this program structure, all Python codes should always start with the keyword "import." Now, what are we importing? Python language is object-oriented. Therefore, it has components of all the Object-Oriented Programming languages. One such property is inheritance or in simple terms, code reuse. The ability to inherit features of codes in Python allows programmers to reuse pieces of codes that had been written elsewhere.

Technically speaking, the import statement tells the Python interpreter to declare classes that have already been used in other Python packages without referring to their full package names. For instance, the statement: "import sys" informs the interpreter to include all the system libraries such as print whenever the Python program is starting.

What does the statement "def main ( ):" mean?

Whenever a Python program is loaded and executed, the computer's memory—the Random Access Memory—contains the objects with function definitions. The function definitions provide the programmers with the capabilities of instructing the control unit to place the function object into the appropriate section of the computer's memory. In other words, it's like instructing the control unit to check the main memory and initialize the program that needs to be executed.

The function objects in the memory can be specified using names. That's where the statement "def main ( ):" comes in. It simply tells the control unit to start executing the Python code statements that are placed immediately after the statement "def main ( ):"

For example, the Python code below creates a function object and assigns it the name "main":

```
def main ():

    if len (sys.argv) == 10:

        name = sys.argv [2]

    else:

        name = "Introduction to Machine Learning."

    print ("Hello"), name
```

In the above code, the Python interpreter will run all the function statements in the Python file by placing the set of functions objects in the memory and linking each of them with the namespace. This will happen when the program is initialized with the import statement.

But more fundamentally, "What are the different elements of Python code?" Well, all Python programs have the following components:

- **Documenting the program.** Any statement in the program (except the first) that starts with "#" is treated as a command line or comment line and will be ignored during execution. This will allow you to comment on sections of the code for proper documentation.

- **Keywords.** The keywords are instructions that the interpreter recognizes and understands. For instance, the word "print" in the earlier program is a keyword. In Python, there are two main types of keywords: the functions and the control keywords. Functions are simple verbs such as print that tell the interpreter what to do while the control keywords control the flow of execution.

- **Modules.** Python program is shipped with a large list of modules that increase its functionality. The modules will help you to organize your code in a manner that's easy to debug and control the code.

- **Program statements.** The program statements are sentences or instructions that tell the control unit to perform a given operation. Unlike most programming languages, the Python statements don't need a semicolon at the end.

- **Whitespace.** The white spaces are a collective name given to tabs, the spaces, and newlines/carriage returns. The Python language is strict on where the white space should be placed in the code.

- **Escape sequences.** The Escape sequences are special characters that are used for output. For instance: the sequence "\n" in the program tells Python to output on a new line.

Python Variables

There's so much that goes on in the main memory of the computer whenever you run a program. Understanding the concept of variables and data types will help you to write efficient programs.

A program is simply a sequence of instructions (statements) that directs your computer to perform a particular task. For instance, the previous program printed the phrase "Hello World! This is my first program" on the screen when it was executed. But before you could see the output on the screen, some data had to be kept in the computer's memory.

The use of data applies to all programming languages—Python included—therefore, understanding the mechanisms of data management in the computer's memory is the first step towards developing robust, efficient, and powerful applications.

A variable can be conceived as a temporary storage location in the computer's main memory and specifically in the Random Access Memory. This temporary storage location is what will hold the data that you would like to use in the program. In other words, the variable location of memory that holds data whenever your program is executing. So, whenever you define a variable, you'll actually be reserving a temporary storage location in the computer's memory.

All the variables that you define must have names and an equivalent data type—a sort of classification of the variable that specifies the type of value the variable should hold. The data types help to specify what sort of mathematical, relational, or even logical operations that you can apply to the variable without causing an error. Ideally, when you assign variables to data types, you can begin to store numbers, characters, and even constants in the computer's main memory.

Since Python language is an oriented programming language, it is not "statically typed." This means that the interpreter regards every variable as an object. Therefore, you have to declare the variables before using them in your program. So, how can you declare variables in Python?

Names or identifiers usually declare Python variables. Just like any other programming languages that you have so far learned, the conventions for naming the variables must strictly be adhered to. Below are some naming conventions that you should follow when declaring variables:

- All variable names should always begin with a letter (A to Z) or an underscore. For instance, "age" is a valid variable name while "–age" isn't a valid variable name.
- Any variable name you declare cannot start with a number. For instance, 9age is not a valid variable name.

- Special symbols shouldn't be used when declaring variable names. For instance, @name isn't allowed as a variable name.
- The maximum number of characters to use for your variable name shouldn't exceed 255.

To reserve a temporary memory location in the name of a variable, you don't have to use the explicit declaration like other programming languages. If you've had experience in other programming languages such as Pascal or C, I am sure you know that declaring a variable explicitly before assigning any value is a must.

In Python, the declaration of variables usually occurs automatically the moment you assign a value to it. For instance, the statement:

age=10

Automatically reserves a temporary storage location in memory space called "age" and assigns 10 to it.

It is also possible to assign a single value to several variables simultaneously. For instance, the statement below reserves temporary memory spaces for 2 variables namely: age and count, and assigns the value 30:

age, count=30

Python language has different categories of data types that are used to define the storage methods and mathematical operations. Below are examples of data types in Python language:

- Numbers
- String
- List
- Tuple
- Dictionary

Numbers

The Number data types stores numeric values. The number of objects will automatically be initialized whenever you assign a specific value to the variable. For instance, the code illustrated below creates 2 variable objects (age and count) and assigns them the values 10 and 30, respectively:

age = 10

count= 30

If you want to delete the reference to the Number object, you'll use the word "del" followed by the variable name that you wish to delete. Consider the code below that deletes two variables: age and count that have already been declared and used."

del age, count

Python language supports four different categories of number types. These are:

- int. when used in a declaration, it refers to signed integers. These include those whole numbers that range from 8 bits to 32 bits.
- Long. These are long integers. They can be represented either in octal and hexadecimal numbering notation.
- float. These are floating real point values. They may range from 8 bits to 64 bits long.
- Complex. These are complex numbers.

Strings

Strings are stored as consecutive sets of characters in the computer's memory locations. Python language allows you to use either pair of single or double quotes when defining the strings. Other subsets of string variable types can be specified using the slice operator ([ ] and the [:]) with the indexes that range from 0 at the beginning of the string. The plus (+) operator performs string concatenation (joining of two or more strings) while the asterisk (*) operator performs string repetition.

CHAPTER 20:

Numbers and Operators

S ince it is called a "computer," mathematical calculation, of course, is the basic computer skill. The operations in Python are simple and intuitive. Open up the Python Command Line, type in the following numeric operation, and you're ready to run it:

Numbers

Numbers are used for storing values, which are numeric. We create them by assigning some value to them. See the example given below:

number1 = 5

number2 = 20

When you call the variable "number1," you will get 5, and if you call variable "number2," you will get 20 as the result. This is shown below:

number1 = 5

number2 = 20

print (number1)

print (number2)

The program will give the following result:

Mathematical Operators

1) Addition

>>>4 + 2

2) Subtraction

>>>4 - 2

3) Multiplication

>>>4 * 2

4) Division

>>>4 / 2

5) Remainder

>>>4 % 2

With these basic operations, we can use Python as if we were using a calculator. Take buying a house. A property costs 20000 dollars and is subject to a 5% tax on the purchase, plus a 10% down payment to the bank. Then, we can use the following code to calculate the amount of cash to be prepared:

>>>20000*(0.5+ 0.1)

In addition to the usual numeric operations, strings can also be added. The effect is to concatenate two strings into one character.

String

Input:

>>>" I am a follower of " + "Christianity"

Output:

I am a follower of Christianity

Input:

>>>"Example" *2

Output:

Example

Multiplying a string by an integer n repeats the string n times.

Comparison Operator

Python uses comparison operators like ==, >, and < in its program. Below, we will explain with an example.

Program code is below:

first = 34

second = 44

if (first > second)

print "First one is larger"

else

print "Second one is larger"

Output is:

Second one is larger

Logical Operators

In addition to numerical operations, computers can also perform logical operations. It's easy to understand the logic if you've played a killing game or enjoyed a detective story. Like Sherlock Holmes, we use logic to determine whether a statement is true or false. A hypothetical statement is called a proposition, such as "player A is a killer." The task of logic is to find out whether a proposition is true or false.

Computers use the binary system, where they record data in zeros and ones. There are technical reasons why computers use binary. Many of the components that make up a computer can only represent two states, such as the on and off of a circuit, or the high and low voltages. The resulting system is also relatively stable. If you use the decimal system, some computer components will have 10 states, such as the voltage into 10 files. That way, the system becomes complex and error-prone. In Binary Systems, 1 and 0 can be used to represent the true and false states. In Python, we use the keywords True and False to indicate True and False. Data such as True and False are called Boolean values.

Sometimes, we need further logical operations to determine whether a complex proposition is true or false. For example, in the first round, I learned that "player A is not a killer" is true, and in the second round, I learned that "player B is not a killer" is true. So, in the third round, if someone says, "player A is not a killer, and player B is not a killer," then that person is telling the truth. If the two propositions connected by "and" are respectively true, then the whole proposition is true. Virtually, we have a "and" of the logical operation.

In the operation, when both sub propositions must be true, the compound proposition connected by and is true. The "and" operation is like two bridges in a row. You must have both bridges open to cross the river. Take, for example, the proposition that China is in Asia and

Britain is in Asia. The proposition that Britain is in Asia is false, so the whole proposition is false. In Python, we use and for the logical operation of and.

>>>True and True # True

>>>False and True # false

>>>False and False # True

We can also compound the two propositions with "or." Or is humbler than an aggressive "and." In the phrase "China is in Asia, or Britain is in Asia," for example, the speaker leaves himself room. Since the first half of this sentence is true, the whole proposition is true. "Or" corresponds to the "or" logic operation.

In the "or" operation, as long as there is a proposition for true, then "or" connected to the compound proposition is true. The "or" operation is like two bridges crossing the river in parallel. If either bridge is clear, pedestrians can cross the river.

The above logic operation seems to be just some life experience and does not need a computer such as complex tools. With the addition of a judgment expression, a logical operation can really show its power.

Operator Precedence

If there is more than one operator in an expression, consider the precedence of the operation. Different operators have different precedence. Operators can be grouped in order of precedence. Below is the list of operator precedence in an order.

Exponent powers have the highest precedence, followed by the mathematical operator multiplication, division, addition, and subtraction. And the next comes Bitwise operators followed by logical operators at the end.

CHAPTER 21:

Operators in Python

Y ou will realize that some program requests specific information or show the text on the screen. Sometimes we start the program code by informing the readers about our programs. To make things look easy for the other coders, it is important to give it the name or title that is simple and descriptive.

As a programmer, you can use a string literal that comprises the print function to get the right data. String literal is a line of the text surrounded by the quotes. They can be either double or single quotes. Although the type of quotes a programmer use matters less, the programmer must end with the quotes that he/she has used at the beginning of the phrase. You can command your computer to display a phrase or a word on the screen by just doing as mentioned above.

Files

Apart from using the print function to obtain a string when printing on the screen, it can be used to write something onto the file. First, you will have to open up the myfile.txt and write on it before assigning it the file, which is a variable. Once you have completed the first step, you will have to assign "w" in the new line to tell the program that you will only write or make changes after the file has opened. It is not mandatory to use print function; just use the right methods like read method.

Read method is used to open specific files to help you read the available data. You can use this option to open a specific file. Generally, the read method helps the programmers to read the contents into variable data, making it easy for them to open the program they would like to read.

Integers

Always make sure that the integers are kept as whole numbers if you are using them. They can be negative or positive only if there are no decimals. However, if your number has a decimal point, use it as a floating number. Python will automatically display such integers on the screen.

Moreover, you cannot place one number next to others if you are using the integers because Python is a strongly typed language; thus, it will not recognize them when you use them together. However, you put both the number and the string together by making sure you turn the number into a string first before going to the next steps.

Triple Quotes

After reading and understanding both the single and double quotes, it is now time to look at the triple quotes. The triple quotes are used to define the literal that spans many lines. You can use three singles, double, or single when defining an authentic.

Strings

Although a string is seen as a complicated thing to many beginners, it is a term used by the programmers when referring to a sequence of characters and works just like a list. A string contains more functionality, which is specific than a list. You will find it challenging to format the strings when writing out the code because some messages will not be fixed easily due to its functionality. String formatting is the only way to go away within such a situation.

Escape Sequences

They are used to donate special characters which are hard to type on the keyboard or those that can be reserved to avoid confusion that may occur in programming.

Operator Precedence

It will help you to track what you are doing in Python. In fact, it makes things easy when ordering the operation to receive the right information. So, take enough time to understand how the operator precedence works to avoid confusion.

Variables

Variables refer to the labels donated somewhere in the computer memory to store something like holding values and numbers. In the programming typed statistically, the variables have predetermined values. However, Python enables you to use one variable to store many different types. For example, in the calculator, variables are like memory function to hold values that can be retrieved in case you need them later. The variables can only be erased if you store them in the newer value. You will have to name the variable and ensure it has an integer value. Moreover, the programmer can define a variable in Python by providing the label value. For instance, a programmer can name a variable count and even make it an integer of one, and this can be written as; count=1. It allows you to assign the same name to the variable, and in fact, the Python interpreter cannot read through the information if you are trying to access values in the undefined variable. It will display a message showing syntax error. Also, Python provides you with the opportunity of defining different variables in one line even though this not a good according to our experience.

The Scope of a Variable

It is not easy to access everything in Python, and there will be differences in the length of the variables. However, the way we define the variable plays a vital role in determining the location and the duration of accessing the variables. The part of the program that allows you to access the variable is called the Scope, while the time taken for accessing the variable is a lifetime.

Global variables refer to the variables defined in the primary file body. These variables are visible throughout the file and also in the file that imports specific data. As such, these variables cause a long-term impact, which you may notice when working on your program. This is the reason why it is not good to use global variables in the Python program. We advise programmers to add stuff into the global namespace only if they plan to use them internationally. A local variable is a variable defined within another variable. You can access local variables from the region they are assigned. Also, the variables are available in the specific parts of the program.

Modifying Values

For many programming languages, it is easy for an individual to define a particular variable whose values have been set. The values which cannot be modified or changed in the programming language, are called constants. Although this kind of restrictions are not allowed in Python, they are used to ensure some variables are marked, indicating that no one should change those values. You must write the name in capital letters, separated with underscores. A good example is shown below.

NUMBER_OF_HOURS_IN_A_DAY=24

It is not mandatory to put the correct number at the end. Since Python programming does not keep tracking and has no rules for inserting the correct value at the end, you are free and allowed to say, for example, that they are 25 hours in a day. However, it is important to put the correct value for other coders to use in case they want.

Modifying values is essential in your string as it allows a programmer to change the maximum number in the future. Therefore, understanding the working of the string in the program contributes a lot to the success of your program. One has to learn and know where to store the values, the rules governing each value, and how to make them perform well in a specific area.

The Assignment Operator

We had not given it the specific name. It refers to an equal sign (=). You will be using the assignment operator to assign values to the variable located at the left side on the right of the statement. However, you must evaluate if the value on the right side is an arithmetic expression. Note that the assignment operator is not a mathematical sign in the programming because, in programming, we are allowed to add all types of things and make them look like they are equivalent to a certain number. This sign is used to show that those items can be changed or turned into the part on the other side.

CHAPTER 22:

Essential Libraries for Machine Learning in Python

Many developers nowadays prefer the usage of Python in their data analysis. Python is not only applied in data analysis but also in statistical techniques. Scientists, especially the ones dealing with data, also prefer using Python in data integration. That's the integration of Web apps and other environment productions.

The features of Python have helped scientists to use it in Machine Learning. Examples of these qualities include consistent syntax, being flexible, and even having a shorter time in development. It also has the ability to develop sophisticated models and has engines that could help in predictions.

As a result, Python boasts of having a series or set of very extensive libraries. Remember, libraries refer to a series of routines and sorts of functions with different languages. Therefore, a robust library can lead to tackling more complex tasks. However, this is possible without writing several code lines again. It is good to note that Machine Learning relies majorly on mathematics. That's mathematical optimization, elements of probability, and also statistical data. Therefore, Python comes in with a rich knowledge of performing complex tasks without much involvement.

The following are examples of essential libraries used in our present.

Scikit–learn

Scikit-learn is one of the best and a trendy library in Machine Learning. It has the ability to supporting learning algorithms, especially the unsupervised and supervised ones.

Examples of Scikit learn include the following.

- K-means
- Decision trees
- Linear and logistic regressions and also
- Clustering

This kind of library has major components from NumPy and SciPy. Scikit-learn has the power to add algorithms sets, that are useful in Machine Learning and also tasks related to data mining. That's, it helps in classification, clustering, and even regression analysis. There are also other tasks that this library can efficiently deliver. A good example includes ensemble methods, feature selection, and more so, data transformation. It is good to understand that the pioneers or experts can easily apply this if at all, they can be able to implement the complex and sophisticated parts of the algorithms.

TensorFlow

It is a form of algorithm which involves deep learning. They are not always necessary, but one good thing about them is their ability to give out correct results when done right. It will also enable you to run your data in a CPU or GPU. That's, you can write data in the Python program, compile it then run it on your central processing unit. Therefore, this gives you an easy time in performing your analysis. Again, there is no need for having these pieces of information written at C++ or instead of other levels such as CUDA.

TensorFlow uses nodes, especially the multi-layered ones. The nodes perform several tasks within the system, which include employing networks such as artificial neutral, training, and even set up a high volume of datasets. Several search engines such as Google depend on this type of library. One main application of this is the identification of objects. Again, it helps in different Apps that deal with the recognition of voice.

Theano

Theano also forms a significant part of Python library. Its vital tasks here are to help with anything related to numerical computation. We can also relate it to NumPy. It plays other roles such as:

- Definition of mathematical expressions
- Assists in the optimization of mathematical calculation
- Promotes the evaluation of expressions related to numerical analysis.

The main objective of Theano is to give out efficient results. It is a faster Python library as it can perform calculations of intensive data up to 100 times. Therefore, it is good to note that Theano works best with GPU as compared to the CPU of a computer. In most industries, the CEO and other personnel use Theano for Deep Learning. Also, they use it for computing complex and sophisticated tasks. All these became possible due to its processing speed. Due to the expansion of industries with a high demand for data computation techniques, many people are opting for the latest version of this library. Remember, the latest one came to limelight some years back. The new version of Theano, that's version 1.0.0, had several improvements, interface changes, and composed of new features.

Pandas

Pandas is a library that is very popular and helps in the provisions of data structures that are of high level and quality. The data provided here is simple and easy to use. Again, it's intuitive. It is composed of various sophisticated inbuilt methods, which make it capable of performing tasks such as grouping and timing analysis. Another function is that it helps in a combination of data and also offering filtering options. Pandas can collect data from other sources such as Excel, CSV, and even SQL databases. It also can manipulate the collected data to undertake its operational roles within the industries. Pandas consist of two structures that enable it to perform its functions correctly. That's Series which has only one dimensional, and data frames which boast of two dimensional. Pandas has been regarded as the most strong and powerful Python library over the time being. Its main function is to help in data manipulation. Also, it has the power to export or import a wide range of data. It is applicable in various sectors, such as in the field of data science.

Pandas is effective in the following areas:

- Splitting of data
- Merging of two or more types of data
- Aggregating of data
- Selecting or subsetting of data and
- Data reshaping

Diagrammatic explanations

Series Dimensional

SERIES

A	7
B	8
C	9
D	3
E	6
F	9

Data Frames dimensional

DATA FRAME

	A	B	C	D
*0	0	0	0	0
*1	7	8	9	3
*2	14	16	18	6
*3	21	24	27	9
*4	28	32	36	12
*5	35	40	45	15

Applications of pandas in a real-life situation will enable you to perform the following:

- You can quickly delete some columns or even add some texts found within the Dataframe

- It will help you in data conversion

- Pandas can reassure you of getting the misplaced or missing data

- It has a powerful ability, especially in the grouping of other programs, according to their functionality.

Matplotlib

This is another sophisticated and helpful data analysis technique that helps in data visualization. Its main objective is to advise the industry where it stands using the various inputs. You will realize that your production goals are meaningless when you fail to share them with different stakeholders. To perform this, Matplotlib comes in handy with the types of computation analysis required. Therefore, it is the only Python library that every scientist, especially the ones dealing with data prefers. This type of library has good looks when it comes to graphics and images. More so, many prefer using it in creating various graphs for data analyzation. However, the technological world has completely changed with new advanced libraries flooding the industry.

It is also flexible, and due to this, you are capable of making several graphs that you may need. It only requires a few commands to perform this.

In this Python library, you can create various diverse graphs, charts of all kinds, several histograms, and even scatterplots. You can also make non-Cartesian charts too using the same principle.

Diagrammatic explanations

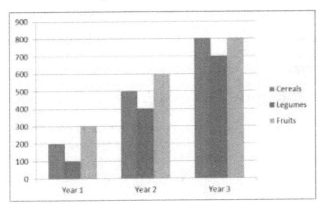

The above graph highlights the overall production of a company within three years. It specifically demonstrates the usage of Matplotlib in data analysis. By looking at the diagram, you will realize that the production was high as compared to the other two years. Again, the company tends to perform in the production of fruits since it was leading in both years 1 and 2 with a tie in year 3. From the figure, you realize that your work of presentation, representation, and even analyzation has been made easier as a result of using this library. This Python library will eventually enable you to come up with good graphics images, accurate data, and much more. With the help of this Python library, you will be able to note down the year your production was high, thus, being in a position to maintain the high productivity season.

It is good to note that this library can export graphics and can change these graphics into PDF, GIF, and so on. In summary, on this library, the following tasks can be undertaken with much ease. They include:

- Formation of line plots
- Scattering of plots
- Creations of beautiful bar charts and building up of histograms
- Application of various pie charts within the industry
- Stemming the schemes for data analysis and computations
- Being bin a position to follow up contours plots
- Usage of spectrograms and lastly
- Quiver plots creation.

Seaborn

Seaborn is also among the popular libraries within the Python category. Its main objective here is to help in visualization. It is important to note that this library borrows its foundation from Matplotlib. Due to its higher level, it is capable of various plots generation such as the production of heat maps, processing of violin plots, and also helping in generation of time series plots.

Diagrammatic Illustrations

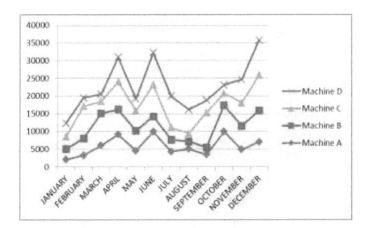

The above line graph clearly shows the performance of different machines the company is using. Following the diagram above, you can eventually deduce and make a conclusion on which machines the company can keep using to get the maximum yield. On most occasions, this evaluation method by the help of Seaborn library will enable you to predict the exact abilities of your different inputs. Again, this information can actually help for future reference in the case of purchasing more machines. Seaborn library also has the power to detect the performance of other variable inputs within the company. For example, the number of workers within the company can be easily identified with their corresponding working rate.

NumPy

This is a very widely used Python library. Its features enable it to perform multidimensional array processing. Also, it helps in the matrix processing. However, these are only possible with the help of an extensive collection of mathematical functions. It is important to note that this Python library is highly useful in solving the most significant computations within the scientific sector. Again, NumPy is also applicable in areas such as linear algebra, derivation of random number abilities used within industries, and more so Fourier transformation. NumPy is also used by other high-end Python libraries such as TensorFlow for Tensors manipulation. In short, NumPy is mainly for calculations and data storage. You can also export or load data to Python since it has those features that enable it to perform these functions. It is also good to note that this Python library is also known as numerical Python.

CHAPTER 23:

How Can Python Work With Machine Learning

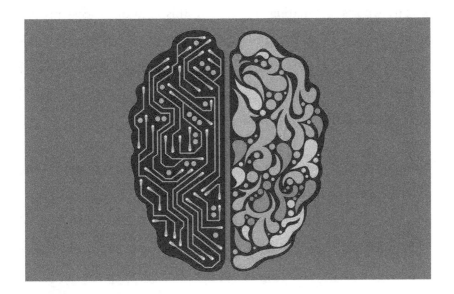

When it comes to completing your own modules and algorithms in Machine Learning, you will find that there is just one language that can help you get it all done. Sure, other programmers may spend time talking about how another language is the best, but Python has the libraries and extensions, the features, the ease of use, and all of the power that you are looking for all in one place. There are so many reasons why you should choose to work with Python when you want to undertake a project that has Machine Learning, and we are going to explore some of those benefits here.

Python has the libraries that you need to handle your Machine Learning algorithms and get things done. We will take a look at some of the libraries that you are able to work with when it comes to the Python language and Machine Learning or data science in a bit. But there are quite a few that you can focus your attention on. This is great news for someone who is just getting started with this kind of process because you are certain to find the library that works the best for your needs. You can find Python libraries that work for all parts of the data analysis and Machine Learning process, from gathering up the data you need all the way to show the visuals at the end.

Python has a lot of power behind it that will ensure that we can get some of our data analysis modules done and ready to go. While we have spent some time talking about how easy Python is to learn and how all programmers can figure this one out, whether you are someone who is just getting started with coding or you have been doing it for a long time with other languages. Even though this is a simple language that we are able to learn and that we can catch onto quickly, that doesn't mean that we will have to give up on some of the power that is necessary for some of the coding we want to complete.

As you can imagine, Machine Learning is going to require some power in order to be successful. If you go in with a wimpy language that is not able to handle complex coding and more, you are going to end up with a lot of issues along the way. This is not a problem that you need to worry about with Python. Despite the ease of using and learning, you will find that this language still has all of the power and strength that you are looking for in order to get all of the different algorithms and modules that you want with Machine Learning done.

The Python language is easy enough to work with that even a beginner is able to learn even some of the more complicated parts that come with Machine Learning. If you have never done coding and this is the first step that you have taken to work on Machine Learning and making it work for you, it may seem like this is all too complicated to handle. But as you go through some of the coding that we have talked about already in this guidebook, and use that to help with Machine Learning and creating some of your own codes in the process, then you will quickly see that it is not as hard or as scary as you may have thought. Python will make all of this easier to handle.

Many of the algorithms that we will use to handle our data and make it do what we would like in the process work the best with the simple and easy to understand codes of Python. We already know that Python is going to come with a really easy to use and read code, and this can be beneficial when we are working with some of the more complicated parts that come with Machine Learning. It can be reassuring to see these recognizable codes in Python when we have to handle our own data analysis, and learning some of the simplicity that comes with Python can help prepare us for some of the work that we need to do with Machine Learning.

Python is also able to work with a lot of the other coding languages out there. With some of our data analysis libraries, we will find that it is best to execute the work with another language. But because Python is able to handle doing some of the work, and it is compatible with other languages, we can still use the Python language in order to help out with writing the codes, but then switching it over, with the help of the Python library that we choose like TensorFlow, in order to have the stronger language finish things up.

The good news here is that the Python language is able to handle a lot of the work and the algorithms that you want to do with Machine Learning. And many times, you will not need to go through and make any adjustments or add Python to another language to get the work done. This makes it so much easier for us to write out the modules we want, while also training and testing them, to ensure that we can work with the data and really understand what it is trying to tell us.

Python is able to handle all of the different parts that come with Machine Learning and good data analysis. As we go through the idea of data analysis, you will find that there are actually a number of steps that need to be followed in order to figure out what is inside of all that data. For example, you will need to gather and sort through the data, you will need to clean it up and deal with all of the different parts that are there, and you will need to consider which algorithms to use and then train and test it.

All of this needs to be done before we are even able to put the data through and do the analysis. Then, when we get to the analysis, we may need to trial and error again to make sure that it is working the way that we want, and then we can use Python again in order to create some of the algorithms that we want with our analysis. All of these steps are important to the process of data analysis and will ensure that you are able to get the information that you need, and you can definitely work with Python in order to make this happen.

There may be other choices that we can make when it is time to handle Machine Learning and all that it entails, but you will find that one of the best languages out there that are able to handle all of the work, from finding and gathering the data to cleaning it off to getting the module done, and so much more, you will find that the Python language is able to take on the work.

CHAPTER 24:

Machine Learning and Data Science

What is a Data Scientist?

The funny thing is that this great value of the data contrasts with that precisely the data is the most abundant resource on the planet (it is estimated that 2.5 trillion bytes of new information is created per day). They don't seem easy to make things compatible. How is it possible that something so abundant is so valuable? Even if it was pure supply and demand, accumulating data should be trivial. And the complex thing is to process them.

Until relatively recently, we simply couldn't do it. At the end of the 90s, the field of Machine Learning began to take on an autonomous entity, our ability to work with immense amounts of data was reduced and the social irruption of the internet did the rest. For a few years, we have faced the first great 'democratization' of these techniques. And with that, the boom of data scientists: nobody wants to have an untapped gold mine.

In Search of a Data Scientist

The problem is that, suddenly, there has been a great demand for a profile that, until now, practically did not exist. Remember that you need statistical knowledge that a programmer does not usually have, and computer knowledge that a statistician does not usually even imagine.

Most of the time, it has been solved with self-taught training that completes the basic skills that the training program should have but does not have. That is why, today, we can find a great diversity of professional profiles in the world of data science. According to Burtch Works, 32% of active data scientists come from the world of mathematics and statistics, 19% from computer engineering, and 16% from other engineering.

How to Train

Degrees

Today, there are some double degrees in computer engineering and mathematics (Autonomous University of Madrid, Granada, Polytechnic University of Madrid, Polytechnic University of Catalonia, and Complutense, Murcia Autonomous University of Barcelona) or in computer science and statistics (University of Valladolid) that seem the best option if we consider this specialization.

Postgraduate

The postgraduate is a very diverse world. We can find postgraduate, masters, or specialization courses in almost all universities and a truly excessive private offer.

To give some examples, we have postgraduate degrees at the UGR, the UAB, the UAM, the UPM, or the Pompeu Fabra. However, in postgraduate course, it is more difficult to recommend a specific course.

What we can find in the postgraduate training that we cannot find in the previous training is the 'business orientation' component.

We must not forget that most of the work of data scientists is in companies that seek to make their databases profitable, because what market orientation is highly recommended.

In fact, many of the masters in 'big data' are offered by business schools such as OEI or Institute Empress.

MOOCs

One of the most interesting resources you can find are the MOOCs (you know, the Massive Open Online Courses). In fact, recently, we saw that this self-training option could have a lot of future.

Starting with the specialization program in Big Data of Coursera, we can find online courses from the best universities in the world, all this without mentioning the numerous tools to learn languages like Python or R.

What Languages Should Be Learned?

In reality, as any initiate knows, in programming the choice of one language or another is always complicated. In this election, they intervene from technical or formative factors to simple personal preferences. What is clear is that there are some languages more popular than others.

Although common sense tells us that each language is better for certain things, in practice there is a certain rivalry. Personally, I use R, but I usually recommend Python. Not only because it is prettier, but because it is multipurpose and that is always an advantage.

Other tools

A fireproof

- **Excel:** It is not a language and usually does not like those who work with professional data. Or so they say when asked why polls say otherwise: 59% percent of respondents routinely use excel. So, finally, the application of Office spreadsheets is still a lot of war.

The corporate brother and other languages and programs

- Some languages or environments enjoy some success driven by corporate inertia: it is the case of the classic MATLAB but progressively, it is losing weight and use up to only 6%.
- If we examine the surveys, we can find many more languages that obey more particular needs of the practice of data scientists (or the programs they use): Scala (17%),

Slack (10%), Perl (12%), and C # (6%), Mahout (3%), Apache Hadoop (13%) or Java (23%).

- Also, although it is possible that we should talk about them separately, there are many specific programs (free or proprietary) that are used in data science with different uses. For example, we could talk about Tableau, Rapid Miner, or Weka.

The labor market: salaries and opportunities

Salaries, as in general in the world of software development, change a lot depending on the place, the functions, and the employer. However, right now, it is a well-paid expertise. On a general level and according to the annual KdNuggets survey, salaries/incomes average $ 141,000 for freelancers, 107,000 for employees, 90,000 for government workers, or in the non-profit sector; 70,000 dollars for work in universities.

However, these average salaries must be taken with great caution. While the average salary in the United States is between $ 103,000 and $ 131,000, in Western Europe it is between $ 54,000 and $ 82,000. In Spain, we are in similar numbers because, despite our (increasingly smaller) deficit of product companies, we have large companies (especially banks) that have turned in this field.

What differentiates data science from the rest of the development world is perhaps the shortage of professionals. This phenomenon makes salaries relatively inflated and, as more dater profiles appear, they adjust. Therefore, it can be said that it is time to get on the wave of data science.

Within a couple of years, the market will have matured, and the opportunities will be elsewhere.

CHAPTER 25:

Decision Trees

D ecision trees are built similarly to support vector machines, meaning they are a category of supervised Machine Learning algorithms that are capable of solving both regression and classification problems. They are powerful and used when working with a great deal of data.

You need to learn beyond the barebones basics so that you can process large and complex datasets. Furthermore, decision trees are used in creating random forests, which is arguably the most powerful learning algorithm. In this phase, we are going to exclusively focus on decision trees explicitly because of their popular use and efficiency.

An Overview on Decision Trees

Decision trees are essentially a tool that supports a decision that will influence all the other decisions that will be made. This means that everything from the predicted outcomes to consequences and resource usage will be influenced in some way. Take note that decision trees are usually represented in a graph, which can be described as some kind of chart where the training tests appear as a node. For instance, the node can be the toss of a coin, which can have two different results. Furthermore, branches sprout to individually represent the results, and they also have leaves, which are the class labels. Now you see why this algorithm is called a decision tree. The structure resembles an actual tree. As you probably guessed, random forests are exactly what they sound like. They are collections of decision trees, but enough about them.

Decision trees are one of the most powerful supervised learning methods you can use, especially as a beginner. Unlike other more complex algorithms, they are fairly easy to implement and they have a lot to offer. A decision tree can perform any common data science task, and the results you obtain at the end of the training process are highly accurate. With that in mind, let's analyze a few other advantages, as well as disadvantages, to gain a better understanding of their use and implementation.

Let's begin with the positives:

1. Decision trees are simple in design and, therefore, easy to implement even if you are a beginner without a formal education in data science or Machine Learning. The concept behind this algorithm can be summarized with a sort of a formula that follows a common type of programming statement: If this, then that, else that. Furthermore, the results you will obtain are very easy to interpret, especially due to the graphic representation.

2. The second advantage is that a decision tree is one of the most efficient methods in exploring and determining the most important variables, as well as discovering the

connection between then. Also, you can build new features easily to gain better measurements and predictions. Don't forget that data exploration is one of the most important stages in working with data, especially when there is a large number of variables involved. You need to be able to detect the most valuable ones in order to avoid a time-consuming process, and decision trees excel at this.

3. Another benefit of implementing decision trees is the fact that they are excellent at clearing up some of the outliers in your data. Don't forget that outliers are noise that reduces the accuracy of your predictions. In addition, decision trees aren't that strongly affected by noise. In many cases, outliers have such a small impact on this algorithm that you can even choose to ignore them if you don't need to maximize the accuracy scores.

Finally, there's the fact that decision trees can work with both numerical as well as categorical variables. Decision trees, on the other hand, are proven to be versatile and handle a much more varied set of tasks.

As you can see, decision trees are powerful, versatile, and easy to implement, so why should we ever bother using anything else? As usual, nothing is perfect, so let's discuss the negative side of working with this type of algorithm:

1. One of the biggest issues encountered during a decision tree implementation is overfitting. Take note that this algorithm tends to sometimes create very complicated

decision trees that will have issues generalizing data due to their complexity. This is known as over fitting, and it is encountered when implementing other learning algorithms as well, however, not to the same degree. Fortunately, this doesn't mean you should stay away from using decision trees. All you need to do is invest some time to implement certain parameter limitations to reduce the impact of overfitting.

2. Decision trees can have issues with continuous variables. When continuous numerical variables are involved, the decision trees lose a certain amount of information. This problem occurs when the variables are categorized. If you aren't familiar with these variables, a continuous variable can be a value that is set to be within a range of numbers. For example, if people between ages 18 and 26 are considered of student age, then this numerical range becomes a continuous variable because it can hold any value between the declared minimum and maximum.

While some disadvantages can add to additional work in the implementation of decision trees, the advantages still outweigh them by far.

Classification and Regression Trees

Decision trees need to be divided into classification and regression trees. They handle different problems; however, they are similar in some ways since they are both types of decision trees.

Take note that classification decision trees are implemented when there's a categorical dependent variable. On the other side, a regression tree is only implemented in the case of a continuous dependent variable. Furthermore, in the case of a classification tree, the result from the training data is the mode of the total relevant observations. This means that any observations that we cannot define will be predicted based on this value, which represents the observation which we identify most frequently.

Regression trees, on the other hand, work slightly differently. The value that results from the training stage is not the mode value, but the mean of the total observations. This way, the unidentified observations are declared with the mean value, which results from the known observations.

Both types of decision trees undergo a binary split, however, going from the top to bottom. This means that the observations in one area will spawn two branches that are then divided inside the predictor space. This is also known as a greedy approach because the learning algorithm is seeking the most relevant variable in the split while ignoring the future splits that could lead to the development of an even more powerful and accurate decision tree.

As you can see, there are some differences as well as similarities between the two. However, what you should note from all of this is that the splitting is what has the most effect on the accuracy scores of the decision tree implementation. Decision tree nodes are divided into sub-nodes, no matter the type of tree. This tree split is performed to lead to a more uniform set of nodes.

Now that you understand the fundamentals behind decision trees, let's dig a bit deeper into the problem of overfitting.

The Overfitting Problem

You learned earlier that overfitting is one of the main problems when working with decision trees, and sometimes it can have a severe impact on the results. Decision trees can lead to a 100% accuracy score for the training set if we do not impose any limits. However, the major downside here is that overfitting creeps in when the algorithm seeks to eliminate the training errors, but by doing so, it actually increases the testing errors. This imbalance, despite the score, leads to terrible prediction accuracy in the result. Why does this happen? In this case, the decision trees grow many branches, and that's the cause of overfitting. To solve this use, you need to impose limitations on how much the decision tree can develop and how many branches it can spawn. Furthermore, you can also prune the tree to keep it under control, much like how you would do with a real tree in order to make sure it produces plenty of fruit.

To limit the size of the decision tree, you need to determine new parameters during the definition of the tree. Let's analyze these parameters:

1. **min_samples_split:** The first thing you can do is change this parameter to specify how many observations a node will require to be able to perform the splitting. You can declare anything with a range of one sample to maximum samples. Just keep in mind that to limit the training model from determining the connections that are very common to a particular decision tree, you need to increase the value. In other words, you can limit the decision tree with higher values.

2. **min_samples_leaf:** This is the parameter you need to tweak to determine how many observations are required by a node, or in other words, a leaf. The overfitting control mechanism works the same way as for the samples split parameter.

3. **max_features:** Adjust this parameter in order to control the features that are selected randomly. These features are the ones that are used to perform the best split. To determine the most efficient value, you should calculate the square root of the total features. Just keep in mind that in this case, the higher value tends to lead to the overfitting problem we are trying to fix. Therefore, you should experiment with the value you set. Furthermore, not all

cases are the same. Sometimes a higher value will work without resulting in overfitting.

4. **max_depth:** Finally, we have the depth parameter, which consists of the depth value of the decision tree. To limit the overfitting problem, however, we are only interested in the maximum depth value. Take note that a high value translates to a high number of splits, therefore a high amount of information. By tweaking this value, you will have control over how the training model learns the connections in a sample.

Modifying these parameters is only one aspect of gaining control of our decision trees in order to reduce overfitting and boost performance and accuracy. The next step after applying these limits is to prune the trees. Pruning

This technique might sound too silly to be real; however, it is a legitimate Machine Learning concept that is used to improve your decision tree by nearly eliminating the overfitting issue. As with real trees, what pruning does is reduce the size of the trees in order to focus the resources on providing highly accurate results. However, you should keep in mind that the segments that are pruned are not entirely randomly selected, which is a good thing. The sections that are eliminated are those that don't help with the classification process and don't lead to any performance boosts. Less complex decision trees lead to a better-optimized model.

Conclusion

This is the end of the guidebook. The next milestone is to make the best use of your new-found wisdom of Python programming, Data Science, Data Analysis, and Machine Learning that have resulted in the birth of the powerhouse, which is the "Silicon Valley." So many companies, that span a lot of different industries, are able to benefit when they work with data analysis. This allows them to get a lot of the power and control that they want for their respective industries and will ensure that they will be able to really impress their customers and get some good results in the process. Learning how to use a data analysis is going to change the game in how you do business, as long as it is used in the proper manner.

This guidebook has been organized well to explore what data analysis is all about, and how we are able to use this for our benefits as well. There are a lot of business tools out there, but data analysis is designed to help us focus on finding the hidden patterns and insights that are in our data, making it easier to base our decisions on data, rather than intuition and guessing as we did in the past. And when it comes to making sure that we complete the data analysis in the right manner, nothing is better than working with the Python coding language to get things done.

There are so many aspects that need to come into play when we are working with our own data analysis, and it is important that we take the time to learn how these works, and how to put it all together. And that is exactly what we will do in this guidebook. When you are ready to learn more about Python data analysis, and all of the different parts that come together to help us with understanding our data and how to run our business, make sure to recheck this guide to help you.

Now that you have finished reading this book and mastered the use of Python programming, you are all set to start developing your own Python-based Machine Learning model as well as performing big data analysis using all the open sources readily available and explicitly described in this book. You can position yourself to use your deep knowledge and understanding of all the cutting edge technologies obtained from this book to contribute to the growth of any company and land yourself a new high paying and rewarding job!

Remember, however, – and wherever – you are teaching, foster a good learning environment. Trial and error is all part of learning when it comes to coding. Children like it when adults make mistakes, so when you know that they have a good understanding of what you are teaching them, then you can make mistakes too. Does your child notice this and pick up on it?

If you are working at home with your child, then work together rather than leaving them to play by themselves. If possible, involve other family members, too. Coding doesn't have to be a boring, dry, academic subject. Foster that creativity in your children by being creative yourself. Have fun and enjoy bonding with your child!